Images of Wallace Stevens

To Blanche and Oscar Kessler

Acknowledgments

I am grateful to the Harvard University Library for providing me with efficient services during the writing of this book.

Several members of the Rutgers University faculty read the manuscript and, in various ways, provided encouragement and useful commentary: Paul Fussell, Fred Main, and John McCormick. Undoubtedly my greatest debt, however, is to Horace Hamilton of Rutgers who suggested that I write on Stevens and served as a sound and sympathetic critic during several stages of the project.

Finally, Avis DeVoto deserves credit for making the world an agreeable place in which to work.

CONTENTS

Images of Wallace Stevens

INTRODUCTION

"No mind is more valuable than the images
it contains."

W. B. Yeats, *Essays and Introductions*

"The overpowering vision which matter-of-
fact judgement thus belittles remains in
memory, and escapes the repression of the
intellect to find itself again in the communi-
cated imagery of poetry."

Maud Bodkin, *Archetypal Patterns in Poetry*

What Sainte-Beuve wrote in 1866 about the changes he
had witnessed in the readers of French poetry is appli-
cable to Wallace Stevens' audience:

For us the greatest poet is the one who in his works has given
the reader the most to imagine and to dream about, who has
moved him to be himself a poet. The greatest poet is not the
one whose work is the most accomplished; he is the one who
suggests the most, with whom at first one does not grasp entirely all that he has meant to say and express, and who leaves
one much to ask, to explain, to study, much for one to finish.

A little later in the same essay, Sainte-Beuve announces
what the new reader-critic is looking for in poetry:

The vague, the obscure, the difficult, if they are combined
with some greatness, are what it prefers. It must have material

which it may itself construct and work on. For its own part it is far from displeased at having its skein to untangle, and at being given from time to time, if I may say so, a tricky job to do.[1]

Probably all of the words that the French critic used in describing the Symbolist poets have been used in describing Stevens. He is often "vague," "obscure," "difficult," and he is obsessed by the need to "imagine" and "dream." Unlike Eliot and Pound, who have religious or political ideas to promote and consequently may sometimes subordinate poetry to the uses of poetry, Stevens by employing images *for themselves* resembles the French in their cultivation of pure poetry. The meaning of a Stevens poem resides in the language and is not dependent upon cultural background; he requires no special knowledge from outside the poems, knowledge of history or literature. When the poet says that "the words of things entangle and confuse," he announces the only barrier between himself and his audience.

Stevens' poetry reveals no linear development of the sort that characterizes the works of Yeats or Eliot or more recently Robert Lowell; rather, the poems eddy around certain fixed ideas revealed in a recurring pattern of imagery. The poetry of Yeats and Eliot can be conveniently divided into stages, profitably studied in isolation, and a reader can personally trace the steps that lead to the maturity of the *Four Quartets* or the Crazy Jane poems. Unfortunately for the reader seeking the foothold of stages, there is nothing in Stevens comparable to Eliot's "conversion" or Yeats's volumes *The Green Helmet* and *Responsibilities* in which he moves out of the Celtic Twilight, or the "cultic Twalette," as Joyce called it. Stevens' "maturity is something he started

with," [2] and the poet suffers at the hands of critics who
feel deprived of the road by which he reached maturity.
G. S. Fraser may be typical of Stevens' detractors: he
finds him a "pragmatic solipsist" who fails to change
pace as Eliot does in "The Waste Land." [3] Once Stevens
established his themes in his first volume, *Harmonium,*
he continued to work variations on them, arranging
familiar images into new combinations. No single statement is more crucial to an understanding of Stevens'
method than one he made in a letter to William Carlos
Williams:

My idea is that in order to carry a thing to the extreme necessity [necessary] to have it one has to stick to it. . . . Given a
fixed point of view, realistic, imagistic or what you will, everything adjusts itself to that point of view; and the process of ad-
justment is a world of flux, as it should be for a poet. But to
fidget with points of view leads always to new beginnings and
incessant new beginnings lead to sterility. A single manner
and mood thoroughly matured and exploited is that fresh
thing. . . . [4]

Stevens never tries to "fidget with points of view"; and
like Valéry's musician, he makes "a diversity of variants
or solutions of the same subject." [5] Consequently, a
reliable entry into the poems is by way of images, Stevens' musical notation.

This study, then, is chiefly a discussion of several of
Stevens' major or controlling images, with the intention
of revealing a general pattern. Because, as Stevens
wrote, "One poem proves another and the whole" (CP,
441), I have analyzed images in terms of other images,
and in this method I must admit to sharing the self-
contained world that Fraser finds objectionable. But I
feel that there is need for a study that subordinates, for

the most part, judgments about the quality of poems —
the Stevens canon has yet to be established — and con-
centrates on one poetic means, a study of what is there
on the page, not in the mind of Santayana or the French
Symbolist poets. I have not treated poems as aesthetic
objects whose unity and integrity cannot be violated, but
have used parts of poems (as Stevens used "Parts of a
World") and been willing to devote as much attention to
inferior as to superior works (e.g., *Owl's Clover*) if the
analysis helps to uncover a prevailing pattern. Sometimes a poem that fails because it is contrived can be
useful in exposing the poet's concerns. My own aim is
expressed by Henri Focillon:

It has always seemed to me that in difficult studies of this sort
— studies that are repeatedly exposed both to a vagueness of
judgments respecting actual worth and to extremely ambiguous interpretations — the observation of technical phenomena
not only guaranteed a certain controlled objectivity, but afforded an entrance into the very heart of the problem, *by presenting it to us in the same terms and from the same point of
view as it is presented to the artist.*[6]

I attempt as much as possible to concentrate on one
"technical phenomenon," feeling, with Stevens, that
"the purpose that comes first,/ The surface, is the purpose to be seen . . ." (CP, 531).

Like the imagination-reality opposition, which could
be seen as the single idea underlying all of Stevens'
work, the poems reveal a conflict "between an asceticism tending to kill language by stripping words of all
association and a hedonism tending to kill language by
dissipating their sense in a multiplicity of associations"
(NA, 13). Stevens, for the most part, balances these ex-

tremes and thereby creates new possibilities of expression. His language of the abstract was not discovered late in life but was an essential counterpart to the more celebrated sights and sounds of *Harmonium.* Stevens was always both an ascetic and a hedonist.

The modern distrust of abstract ideas in poetry has caused a number of critics (Randall Jarrell, for example) to feel that Stevens' poems become less effective as his intellect becomes dominant, but I tend to agree with I. A. Richards that "too much importance has always been attached to the sensory qualities of images." [7] Many of Stevens' abstractions, such as "nothingness," are charged with emotion and truly grounded in the particulars of the world, and a late poem like "The Course of a Particular" (OP, 96–97) is filled with images, and articulates an emotional problem that possibly could not be dealt with using images of an acutely sensory nature. Rather than moving away from emotions, the poems may enlarge the range and quality of emotions, as well as our means of expressing them.

The images I discuss are not simply occasional metaphors; they reappear frequently, intensifying and shaping the body of the whole work. By repeating images to evoke associations, Stevens enlarges his metaphors into symbols, if we see a symbol as differing from a metaphor only in degree, in the work-load it is made to carry. Stevens' persistently recurring images constitute a kind of symbolic system, although it is neither rigid nor incapable of contradictions within its framework. North, south, statue, wilderness, music, sea, sun, moon, and various colors are symbols that suggest indefinite and sometimes even contradictory meanings. They are what Susanne Langer calls "art symbols" as distinguished

from "genuine symbols," which are signs or names for
a known meaning. The "art symbol," she says, "cannot
strictly be said to have a meaning; what it does have is
import." [8] This definition, as I will later show, is far more
valuable in understanding Stevens' poetry than one that
demands that images such as north and south be signs
with definite meanings, imposing an order that the poetry cannot always substantiate. If one keeps the symbols
flexible and "indefinite" in meaning, they come closer
to revealing their "import," and one avoids such literal
and limited readings as the following: "One cannot suppress a wish that an older semi-tropical culture, perhaps
Egyptian, had impressed Stevens; the loss of élan and
surprise would have found adequate compensation in a
less frantic struggle to assimilate a novel scene and its
landmarks." [9] As if Stevens' problems were merely geo-
graphical, as if the conflict between imagination and
reality could have been resolved by his moving to Cairo.

The danger of a work of this kind is that in paralleling
the approach of the poet one ends up saying the same
things, only in a duller and more labored way. If Stevens
works a series of variations on a single theme, the critic
may well work variations on variations. As long as poets
are distinguishable from philosophers, however, a study
of imagery seems to be a fundamental way of identifying
the poet. Stevens himself, in a poem that is probably one
of his very last, declares that the image is the only means
a poet has of finding himself, in an age without a working mythology. The poet recognizes the need for myth,
a need for communion with society, but he also recognizes that, as C. Day Lewis said, "the poetic myths are
dead; and the poetic image, which is the myth of the
individual, reigns in their stead." [10]

A Mythology Reflects Its Region

A mythology reflects its region. Here
In Connecticut, we never lived in a time
When mythology was possible — But if we had —
That raises the question of the image's truth.
The image must be of the nature of its creator.
It is the nature of its creator increased,
Heightened. It is he, anew, in a freshened youth
And it is he in the substance of his region,
Wood of his forests and stone out of his fields
Or from under his mountains.   (OP, 118)

I hope that I have not imposed an order on the poetry but have simply arranged Stevens' own images into a shape that reveals "the nature of [their] creator."

The following abbreviations will be used throughout:

CP *The Collected Poems of Wallace Stevens.* (New York: Alfred A. Knopf, Inc., 1954).

NA *The Necessary Angel: Essays on Reality and the Imagination.* (New York: Alfred A. Knopf, Inc., 1951).

OP *Opus Posthumous.* (New York: Alfred A. Knopf, Inc., 1957).

1 NORTH AND SOUTH

"And North and South are an intrinsic couple."

Notes toward a Supreme Fiction

I

The "negative capability" of Stevens made him able to hold conflicting opinions, even contradictory ones. One of the major dichotomies in the poet's work is north and south but, as I hope to show, he creates these two poles to represent the essential duality of man: Simply put, north suggests reason, south suggests elemental feeling or passion. An analogue is Nietzsche's well-known description of the Apollonian-Dionysiac duality in *The Birth of Tragedy*. Stevens' north resembles what Nietzsche calls the *"principium individuationis"* and it is contrasted with the south, where man can forget himself through intoxication with physical life. Like the Greek mind Nietzsche characterizes, Stevens' "Apollonian consciousness was but a thin veil hiding from him the whole Dionysiac realm." [1] Early in his career Stevens

led his mock-hero Crispin to the knowledge that one
does not choose permanently between wilderness and
artistic order, the south of physical sensation and the
north of detached thought, but that one discovers life to
be an alternation between the two, enjoying benefits
from both. The same idea underlies the poet's essays:
"It is not only that the imagination adheres to reality,
but, also, that reality adheres to the imagination and that
the interdependence is essential" (NA, 33). Harmony
results from the marriage of sounds, not their divorce;
the extremes of north and south, of cold and heat, temper the human animal until it approaches its full realization.

The hunger to prove development has caused critics
to read Stevens' "Farewell to Florida" (CP, 117–18),
the poem which begins his second volume, as a permanent rejection of the hedonistic delights of *Harmonium* and a commitment to more pressing social demands. Louis L. Martz, for example, believes that Stevens moves into a distinctly new stage of development
with the publication of *Ideas of Order* in 1936, that the
poet "renounces all that 'Florida' has symbolized in his
earlier poetry: that world of vivid physical apprehension,
where man created within the bounds of the natural order." Moreover, the critic maintains that Stevens decided
to "plunge into the turmoil of the mid-thirties, to engage
it somehow in his poetry."[2] If "Farewell to Florida"
did, in fact, declare a permanent choice of north over
south (with north suggesting austerity and Cartesian
coldness), it would contradict a central Stevens idea:
that life is the interplay of mind and world and that one
never makes categorical choices without suffering severe
limitations. As the poet later writes in *Notes toward a
Supreme Fiction:*

He had to choose. But it was not a choice
Between excluding things. It was not a choice

Between, but of. He chose to include the things
That in each other are included, the whole,
The complicate, the amassing harmony. (CP, 403)

Like Milton, Stevens went about putting the universe into his poems, and although the diction he used to build a poem varied, his universe of lively contradiction and paradox never changed. As Roy Harvey Pearce says, "If the movement in the poems has been away from the descriptive and dramatic towards the discursive and dialectical, this is a part of an immanent necessity rising out of a fixed subject matter and the poet's steadily maturing view of it." [3] When we come to Stevens' last poems of *The Rock* we find that Martz's description of Stevens' earlier world is precisely accurate: "That world of vivid physical apprehension, where man created within the bounds of the natural order." It may be useful to look at the crucial "Farewell to Florida" in some detail before proceeding to an investigation of the north-south polarity.

The poem opens with the image of a snake which the speaker is leaving behind on the shore. The snake, or serpent, embodies Stevens' concept of transience, his perpetually changing self and world. Associated numerous times with the "wilderness" of reality, with Africa (OP, 54) and Yucatan (CP, 31), it represents that which alters yet remains the same, actual as opposed to ideal man. (Crispin sees "serpent-kin" [CP, 32]; the revolutionists who stop for orangeade "sing a song of serpent-kin" [CP, 103]. And the image will be used much later to open *The Auroras of Autumn,* suggesting order

in disorder: "This is form gulping after formlessness . . ."
[CP, 411].[4]) Stevens only puts aside an idea or image,
rarely discards one, and his renunciations are never
final. The wilderness, the vivid blooms, the sun, the
leaves, the sea, the colors are all associated in Stevens'
poems with a physical world evoked by the word "south."

Like other poems in *Harmonium*, "Farewell to Florida" reveals the poet in a bad mood, uncertain before
passion, fearful of being swamped by physical excess.
The sun, consistently praised as the life-giving power,
is too harsh to bear. External nature has been distorted
by desire, the trees are "like bones" and the leaves are
"half sand, half sun." The blooms are "vivid" — Stevens
always uses this word in a favorable way — but he despises them. For the moment, all that is attractive becomes offensive.

That his rejection is not permanent, that the speaker is
not even satisfied with his temporary choice, is supported by the final stanza describing the north toward
which he is moving. In the "dark," the poet sails to a
country that is "leafless and lies in a wintry slime/ Both
of men and clouds, a slime of men in crowds." He is
replacing one world for another, "her South" for "my
North," but the images the poet uses to describe his
land are, if anything, more distasteful than those describing hers. There rests at the heart of the poem Stevens'
characteristic ambivalence. He seeks the cold north
because he can "feel sure" there and be "clear of her
mind," in actuality more body than mind. (The woman
can be seen as an individual or as a figure representing
the complex of feeling associated with the abundant,
fecund, sensual south. The latter is more likely in light
of Stevens' other uses of the female image.) His freedom,
however, is illusory, because he only replaces one re-

striction for another; he is "free" again but, paradoxically, only to "return to the violent mind/ That is their mind, these men, and that will bind/ Me round . . . ." In both worlds he is confined; he has simply substituted a fake violence of thought for the real violence of physical contact and passion. He is shown in the upward swing of his continual cycle (Crispin's "fluctuation between sun and moon") and his choice between south and north, heat and cold, sun and darkness, woman and man is indeed difficult to make because they are all parts of "the complicate, the amassing harmony" that Stevens ultimately desires. The speaker seems to be bolstering his courage, rationalizing, when he says, "How content I shall be in the North to which I sail . . . ." The irony cannot be missed. And the last lines of the poem reveal a man who is bitterly, perhaps passively, submitting to necessity, rather than one who is making an affirmative choice and "plunging into the turmoil of the mid-thirties":

> carry me, misty deck, carry me
> To the cold, go on, high ship, go on, plunge on.

As Michel Benamou has pointed out, "The influence of the French Symbolists on Wallace Stevens has become such a well-established fact that it has also become urgent to qualify, if not to disprove it." Professor Benamou sees a profound difference between Stevens and the diverse poets whose aesthetic theories or poetic practice he is assumed to have adopted completely:

At the center of the French Symbolists' aesthetic, there was a spiritual ordeal demanding of the poet that he spurn, destroy, or discard the created world. In Stevens, poetry was the desire to celebrate, refresh, and restore reality. His aesthetic is not embodied by a sterile woman but by images of fertility and fulfillment.[5]

Unlike the artificial woman devised by Mallarmé or the idealized Madame Sabatier, the "cold majesty of the sterile woman" that Baudelaire worshiped, Stevens' woman is not an ideal but the earth itself. He early identifies woman both with the south, the place or condition in which one lives most intimately with physical sensations, and with summer, its perpetual season. Not an inhabitant of the "visionary" south (CP, 68), she is a part of the actual world that can be enjoyed without explanation or meaning. Baudelaire said that "poetry is what is most real, what is completely true only in *another world. This world, a hieroglyphic dictionary.*"[6] He strove through his "correspondences" to find "les transports de l'esprit et des sens," and his awareness of sin made any enjoyment of the physical world impossible; he dreamed of women in poetry, but possessing them in fact was a source of irritation, even pain. In contrast, Stevens distrusts all poets, metaphysicians, scholars when they try to replace woman by a "gaunt fugitive phantom" (CP, 26) of the mind: "she is as she was, reality,/ The gross, the fecund . . ." (CP, 322). In "Homunculus et La Belle Étoile" (CP, 25–26), he selects a southern setting, the Biscayne sea, for his celebration of the physical; it is the biscay green that provides the light essential for self-realization, a light that "charms philosophers"—and poets as well—out of their abstract thoughts and makes scholars look pitiful in their dark introspection. The woman, as usual, can be found in the actual scene:

It might well be that their mistress
Is no gaunt fugitive phantom.
She might, after all, be a wanton,
Abundantly beautiful, eager,

Fecund,
From whose being by starlight, on sea-coast,
The innermost good of their seeking
Might come in the simplest of speech.

Stevens places in the south of *Harmonium* an image of the great earth mother which will appear in various forms throughout his work. She first appears in "In the Carolinas" (CP, 4–5) as the "timeless mother":

Timeless mother,
How is it that your aspic nipples
For once vent honey?

The pine-tree sweetens my body
The white iris beautifies me.

Man can be renewed and fulfilled by returning to a primitive, elemental condition that civilization has stultified, and because life for the poet is "an affair of places" (OP, 158), not of people, he finds himself expressed in the life of the earth. In this attitude he suggests Wordsworth in his cultural primitivism or one of those men Jung describes who "turn back to the mother of humanity, to the psyche, which was before consciousness existed, and in this way they make contact with the source and regain something of that mysterious and irresistible power which comes from the feeling of being part of the whole." [7] The speaker of "Le Monocle de

Mon Oncle" (CP, 13–18) discovers that "the honey of
heaven may or may not come,/ But that of earth both
comes and goes at once." With the stoic perspectives
of maturity he looks back and remembers "how the
crickets came/ Out of their mother grass, like little
kin . . . ," realizing that the satisfactions of both poetry
and sexual love have proved to be ephemeral aspects of
the earth itself. The distaste for the temporal limitations
of physical love is balanced by the knowledge that love
is also the "verve of earth"; the distaste for poetry as
fanciful diversion is balanced by the knowledge that it
can unite us with the permanent forms of nature. The
speaker's passage through life is related to the flight of
a bird that circles the skies but eventually returns to
earth and "flutters to the ground,/ Grown tired of flight."

Death is intimately involved with the mother image,
and consequently one must accept both before one can
approach a true definition of life. In "Sunday Morning"
(CP, 66–70) Stevens rejects the mythological figure of
Jove because "no mother suckled him, no sweet land
gave/ Large-mannered motions to his mythy mind . . . ."
He chooses instead mortality as origin and end of life:

> Death is the mother of beauty; hence from her,
> Alone, shall come fulfilment to our dreams
> And our desires.   (CP, 68)

By confronting the archetype, one is able to accept the
"earthly" mother as part of something larger, an endless
process of birth and death:

> Death is the mother of beauty, mystical,
> Within whose burning bosom we devise
> Our earthly mothers waiting, sleeplessly.   (CP, 69)

The knowledge of life's tragic end intensifies life's incessant beginnings. As Jung wrote, "Those black waters
of death are the water of life, for death with its cold embrace is the maternal womb, just as the sea devours the
sun but brings it forth again." [8] By linking man so inextricably with the world in which he lives, Stevens makes
the human cycle only a version of the cycle of nature:

> Our nature is her nature. Hence it comes,
> Since by our nature we grow old, earth grows
> The same. We parallel the mother's death. (CP, 107–08)

Like Tennyson's Tithonus the poet accepts the human
condition and asks, in effect, "Why should a man desire
in any way/ To vary from the kindly race of men?" Man
is only defined by his own death, which is a return to
the mother who bore him, "the mother of us all,/ The
earthly mother and the mother of/ The dead" (CP, 432).
The acceptance and resignation advocated by Stevens
is perhaps best represented by the soldier who dies
because he must, whose last words might be "Nous
sommes embarqués dans l'aventure sans aucune sensation dominante, sauf peut-être une acceptation assez
belle de la fatalité . . ." (OP, 11). Man's alienation from
his environment is the source of all of his anxiety and
misery, and "the poverty of dirt" can be accepted once
man realizes that

> It is the earth itself that is humanity . . .
> He is the inhuman son and she,
> She is the fateful mother, whom he does not know.
>   (CP, 454)

One of the tasks that Stevens requires of the poet is to
celebrate the "timeless mother" and to renew man's kin-

ship with her, a union weakened by the dualism of
Platonism and Christianity, as well as by abstract reasoning. In "Meditation Celestial & Terrestrial" (CP,
123–24) the poet starkly contrasts a season of winter's
blue reason with the green wilderness of summer. The
"wild warblers are warbling in the jungle" after a period
in which

> Day after day, throughout the winter,
> We hardened ourselves to live by bluest reason
> In a world of wind and frost . . .

And the poet asks:

> But what are radiant reason and radiant will
> To warblings early in the hilarious trees
> Of summer, the drunken mother?

The prodigal excess of physical life is preferable to the
austerity of the mind—for the moment. Thoughtlessly,
he has found the answer to his needs, with what he later
calls, in *Notes toward a Supreme Fiction,* "Fat girl,
terrestrial, my summer, my night" (CP, 406).

Stevens' female symbol is not, however, limited to
suggestions of the purely physical; he uses it in two
ways, dealing with both the sensuous and the sensual.
In "Infanta Marina" (CP, 7–8), the conflict between the
northern mind and the southern body is suspended or
momentarily resolved. The poet effects an imaginative
identification between human and external nature:

> Her terrace *was* the sand
> And the palms and the twilight.   [My italics]

And a union of mind and body:

She made of the motions of her wrist
The grandiose gestures
Of her thought.

But Stevens cannot accept the ideal of perfected passion;
like Yeats's Crazy Jane, he realizes that "fair and foul
are next of kin," and he cannot long suppress the Venus
Naturalis.[9] The sensual demands of life return and the
poet records the torment of dealing with them in "O
Florida, Venereal Soil" (CP, 47–48).

near

Surrounded by the "dreadful sundry of this world,"
the speaker is aroused by a need to find more than "a
few things for themselves." He seeks meaning beyond
the strictly physical, which can become oppressive with
its monotonous demands. He evokes the "virgin of
boorish births" to rescue him from what Stevens calls
elsewhere "the malady of the quotidian," but "lascivi-
ously as the wind" the archetypal female arrives, bringing more questions than satisfying answers. The speaker
dreams that his "virgin" might be transformed into a
"scholar" who could provide some clear, conscious
knowledge of his "insatiable" desires, "a scholar of
darkness,/ Sequestered over the sea,/ Wearing a clear
tiara . . . ." But the clarity of meaning will not come. The
platonic realm of pure ideas is hidden by cloud and
darkness. The poem ends:

Donna, donna, dark,
Stooping in indigo gown
And cloudy constellations,
Conceal yourself or disclose
Fewest things to the lover—
A hand that bears a thick-leaved fruit,
A pungent bloom against your shade.

The female figure here remains, like desire itself, obscure, a force that resides within the shade of the unconscious. Nevertheless, even though she is uncertain and tormenting, she can be visualized within natural abundance. The "thick-leaved fruit" and "pungent bloom" can replace "the dreadful sundry of this world"; in other words, the imagination can restore us to the delights of the senses, whereas the scholar's rational explanations merely stay "sequestered over the sea."

Stevens addresses the female archetype in different ways. When she is a power rather than an actual being, he allows her to undergo various transformations, never restricting her within time or place. She is his celestial or interior paramour, the muses or "portent" of *Owl's Clover*. The metamorphic method, aiming at intensity rather than clarity, is disturbing to readers looking for signs with known referents. Drawing upon a general archetype from the "collective unconscious," the image is at times deliberately ambiguous or contradictory, as in the opening of "To the One of Fictive Music" (CP, 87–88) where the poet evokes a composite figure rather than a single representative:

> Sister and mother and diviner love,
> And of the sisterhood of the living dead
> Most near, most clear, and of the clearest bloom,
> And of the fragrant mothers the most dear
> And queen, and of diviner love the day
> And flame and summer and sweet fire . . .

Likewise the troublesome opening of "Le Monocle de Mon Oncle" addresses a power, not a person: "Mother of heaven, regina of the clouds,/ O sceptre of the sun, crown of the moon . . . ." (Later in this poem the poet casually reveals that Eve was *one* personification of a greater being: "When you were Eve, its acrid juice was sweet.") This urge to unify, to make composite figures, Jung calls "syncretistic strivings" and quotes a prayer of Lucius to the "Queen of Heaven (the moon)" that resembles a Stevens' apostrophe:

Queen of heaven, whether thou be named Ceres, bountiful mother of earthly fruits, or heavenly Cenus, or Phoebus' sister, or Proserpina, who strikest terror with midnight ululations . . . , thou that with soft feminine brightness dost illume the walls of all cities.[10]

The north, and the rational mind it suggests to Stevens, is certainly no *telos*, no clear image of ultimate value, no Ithaca to end his odyssey into reality. More often it suggests "ivory tower" speculation and sterile self-indulgence that does not achieve any liaison between man and his environment.[11] The value of returning to the northern cold is in discovering its blank screen, a *tabula rasa*, on which the southern reality can be projected, contemplated, and possibly understood. The speaker in "The Auroras of Autumn" (CP, 411–21), for example, finds himself a part of the "white of an aging afternoon." He sees a winter sky with winter clouds. His cabin is white, his flowers are white, and "a cold wind chills the beach." But in suffering the total absence of vital warmth, the man realizes the possibilities inherent in such negation:

> He observes how the north is always enlarging the change,
>
> With its frigid brilliances, its blue-red sweeps
> And gusts of great enkindlings, its polar green,
> The color of ice and fire and solitude.
>   (CP, 412–13)

The intellect is a cold thing to Stevens, and its "polar green" is far different from the body's "point-blank," Guatemalan green. But the north does "enlarge the scene," giving the poet perspective on life and the aesthetic distance needed in order to create the poem of reality. Stevens aims at enjoying the favorable effect of withdrawing at times from the demands of the world. As Jung says, "the two fundamental mechanisms of the psyche, extraversion and introversion, are also to a large extent the normal and appropriate ways of reacting to complexes — extraversion as a means of escaping from the complex into reality, introversion as a means of detaching oneself from external reality through the complex." [12] The body can be understood only by the mind, and the mind can find its expression only in bodily terms. Yet, like every descendant of Plato, Stevens is rarely able to effect that harmonious union of mind and body, and even though he professes in *Notes toward a Supreme Fiction* that "North and South are an intrinsic couple . . ." (CP, 392), they enjoy a relationship that is never final, that is continually being consummated.

Stevens' ambivalent handling of the north-south counters is demonstrated in "Arrival at the Waldorf" (CP, 240–41), a poem that deals with a return to the region of the mind after an excursion into physical reality. The decorous, refined surroundings symbolized by the Waldorf are, in fact, Stevens' world, but he is not content. Having made contact with the raw wilderness of feeling, he comes home to the "wild country of the soul," which is tame by comparison. The speaker's use of the word "wild" seems ironic, revealing a dissatisfaction with the rarefied atmosphere in which he finds himself. Like Prufrock, he inhabits a world of his own making, but not of his choosing, a world

> Where the wild poem is a substitute
> For the woman one loves or ought to love,
> One wild rhapsody a fake for another.

The creative act is poor compensation for the loss of physical contact, and the speaker moves like a ghost down dreamlike halls:

> You touch the hotel the way you touch moonlight
> Or sunlight and you hum and the orchestra
> Hums and you say "The world is a verse,
>
> A generation sealed, men remoter than mountains,
> Women invisible in music and motion and color,"
> After that alien, point-blank, green and actual
>   Guatemala.

The Waldorf becomes, in effect, the ivory tower Stevens is accused of inhabiting, the strictly private quarters of the symbolist poet and dandy who refuses to condescend and join the commonplace. However, one would be misled in seeing Stevens as content with remote men and invisible women, or of believing that the world is only a verse. The poet is as much an alien in the Waldorf as he is in the wilderness of Guatemala; rather, to be more affirmative, he is a man intent on living in both. He would like to be satisfied with the richness of a completely physical life, but "the sustenance of the wilderness/ Does not sustain us in the metropoles" (CP, 142). The external world without the creative intelligence is frightfully barbaric; the interior world without the senses is anemic. The interplay between the two is essential to poetry because "the world about us would be desolate except for the world within us. There is the

same interchange between these two worlds that there
is between one art and another, migratory passings to
and fro, quickenings, Promethean liberations and dis-
coveries" (NA, 169).

In "Two Figures in Dense Violet Night" (CP, 85–86),
Stevens further explores the problem of a man removed
from a southern land and dissatisfied with the effete and
"violet" artifice of his hotel. He misses the elemental
passions, the unaffected language that speaks truly of
natural being. He asks his companion to

> Be the voice of night and Florida in my ear.
> Use dusky words and dusky images.
> Darken your speech.

The hotel, the "moist hand" of his companion, the
proper language are aspects of an overrefined culture
that, in its emphasis on clear forms, ignores the shifting
obscurities of human life. He wishes to introduce the
reality of death into the pretty picture which is his life:

> Say, puerile, that the buzzards crouch on the
>   ridge-pole
> And sleep with one eye watching the stars fall
> Below Key West.

The clarity of northern speech denies the darker, primitive part of man's nature, and the speaker realizes that
the world is both clear and obscure; acutely visible yet
finally unknowable:

> Say that the palms are clear in a total blue,
> Are clear and are obscure; that it is night;
> That the moon shines.

"Two Figures in Dense Violet Night" anticipates "Ar- L
rival at the Waldorf" by fifteen years, but it explores the
same problem: man feels homesick wherever he is.

An endless summer of physical delight generates in
Stevens the same aversion as the "frigid brilliances" of
the northern mind. Several of the poems in *Harmonium*
reveal a dissatisfaction with paradise; in the midst of
summer the poet frequently yearns for contact with the
bare earth that summer only disguises. In "Banal Sojourn" (CP, 62–63) the poet's vacation from austerity
begins to cloy, and he recalls moments "When radiance
came running down, slim through the bareness." Summer can become "like a fat beast, sleepy in mildew,/
Our old bane, green, and bloated . . . ," and the poet
sees that the mask of summer keeps the ear, as well as
the eye, from sharing that cold "bliss of stars." Southern
abundance can breed discontent, the desire to escape
from the "fat beast" into the sanctuary of the mind: "one
has a malady, here, a malady. One feels a malady." The
monotony of human passion, with its incessant demands,
is the thinly disguised subject of many of the poems that
appear to deal with external nature: one tires of hearing
the "same jingle" of wind and water and bird; one
regrets that "there is no spring in Florida . . ." (CP,
112).

The "malady" of the speaker of "Banal Sojourn" is
shared by the "platonic person" in a later poem, "The
Pure Good of Theory" (CP, 329–33). Wishing to be a
creature of pure mind, a "form" outside time, he finds
himself faced with the south on a holiday of physical
activity. Images of the great earth mother in all her
nakedness surround him, making his country of the
mind, by contrast, colorless and thin:

Then came Brazil to nourish the emaciated
Romantic with dreams of her avoirdupois, green glade
Of serpents like z rivers simmering,

Green glade and holiday hotel and world
Of the future, in which the memory had gone
From everything, flying the flag of the nude.

This Eden of the senses could be the environment he
seeks, but unfortunately he brings the serpent—his
questioning mind—with him, "the torment of fastidious
thought" (CP, 37). He doubts that happiness can ever
be found exclusively in bodily satisfactions, and his
doubts breed discontent. He falls ill,

Ill of a question like a malady,
Ill of a constant question in his thought,
Unhappy about the sense of happiness.

Was it that—a sense and beyond intelligence?

Having discovered that there can be "a soul in the
world" as well as out of it, the speaker is unsatisfied
by the "fat Elysia" of the south. Just as Stevens is an
alien in the south, his speaker in Brazil is "a Jew from
Europe or might have been." Like Wordsworth, the poet
realizes that the world is too much with us, that culture
and civilization can preclude us from a spontaneous
enjoyment of what is ours by nature.

Despite Stevens' equivocation in dealing with the
images of north and south, there seems little doubt that,
by bringing the imagery of the senses to the level of
consciousness, he hopes to incorporate the two. As a
man, he would be a sensualist; as a poet, he is con-

tinually looking at himself being a sensualist. In "Floral Decorations for Bananas" (CP, 53–54), Stevens focuses on an image from the tropical world, always closely allied in his mind with sensuality. The proper ladies, who have introduced the barbaric fruit into the conventional northern decor, are confronted by an "improper" reality so persistent that all disguises of form fail. The eglantine with which the "women of primrose and purl" wish to decorate crude bananas is inappropriate, hence a distortion of reality. The fruit remains itself, like the fruit which "The Comedian as the Letter C" cannot disguise by metaphor, "good fat, guzzly fruit" (CP, 41).

Critics who insist on Stevens as dandy find it difficult to read this poem without transforming it into a lament for the lost elegance of the eighteenth century. Although Stevens would seem to agree with Pope that *"True Wit* is *Nature* to Advantage drest," he refuses to limit himself to one kind of decorum. Daniel Fuchs insists that

We are concerned in this poem, a typical dandiacal concern, with a matter of dress. Proper attire, that is properly dazzling, is so much an understood matter in the dandy's world that even bananas have apposite dress. Without it they are arrant commoners—insolent, sullen, ignobly shaped, blunt—an insult to the elegantly coifed women.[13]

And John J. Enck feels that the speaker is "a sated man who recoils in distaste from an external excess," a man who "deliberately exaggerates the lurid bananas to establish his own discernment."[14] These readings miss the poet's irony in describing the world of northern artifice, which is petty and sterile in comparison with the raw vitality, the "blunt yellow" of the bananas:

> You should have had plums tonight,
> In an eighteenth-century dish,
> And pettifogging buds,
> For the women of primrose and purl,
> Each one in her decent curl.
> Good God! What a precious light!

Stevens here uses words such as "pettifogging" and "decent" to suggest the loss of animal vitality suffered by a highly decorous society, the human animal in a cage of form. And his use of "precious" (with overtones of the French *précieuse?*) at least makes possible an ambiguous attitude. Like Henry James, Stevens is sometimes accused of promoting the characteristics of society he is exposing.

Even ignoring the possibility of an ironic tone in the earlier stanzas, it would still be difficult to hear the final stanza spoken by a man who "recoils in distaste from external excess." The images are from that vast reservoir of the south, suggesting the element from which man draws his deepest power:

> And deck the bananas in leaves
> Plucked from the carib trees,
> Fibrous and dangling down,
> Oozing cantankerous gum
> Out of their purple maws,
> Darting out of their purple craws
> Their musky and tingling tongues.

The ending of the poem affirms the physical by means of vivid verbs and participles (oozing, dangling, tingling), which communicate a sense of life that is strongly sensual. The poem resembles Theodore Roethke's "Root Cellar" :

Nothing would sleep in that cellar, dank as a ditch,
Bulbs broke out of boxes hunting for chinks in the dark,
Shoots dangled and drooped,
Lolling obscenely from mildewed crates,
Hung down long yellow evil necks, like tropical snakes.
And what a congress of stinks!—
Roots ripe as old bait,
Pulpy stems, rank, silo-rich,
Leaf-mould, manure, lime, piled high against slippery planks.
Nothing would give up life:
Even the dirt kept breathing a small breath.[15]

Life cannot be contained, both poems assert; but whereas
Roethke gives the illusion of being submerged in the
physical, Stevens maintains his aesthetic distance, demanding the right context for the bananas' excess. Like
his persona, Crispin, he would arrange *appropriate* celebration for all things of this world:

> The melon should have apposite *ritual*,
> Performed in verd apparel, and the peach,
> When its black branches came to bud, belle day,
> Should have an *incantation*. And again,
> When piled on salvers its aroma steeped
> The summer, it should have a *sacrament*
> And *celebration*.   (CP, 39)   [My italics]

Just as the mind elevates animal sex to civilized behavior
through the ceremony of marriage, Stevens strives to
provide the sacrament of language that will enhance the
individuality of all natural things. Only death is "absolute and without memorial" (CP, 97), consequently
without a sacrament, because Stevens' vision excludes
the possibility of an afterlife. Susanna's music makes a
"constant sacrament of praise" for the living world, and

in its "immortality" defeats death's "ironic scraping" (CP, 92). To claim that Stevens is a dandy who adheres to a religion of the artificial is to ignore the whole area of imagery centering on the south. His range of experience includes both the natural and the artificial and, unlike the Yeats of "Sailing to Byzantium," he does not reject the "fish, flesh, and fowl," but enjoys the "sensual music" that every dandy from Brummel to Beerbohm would find indecorous, if not offensive.

But Stevens the poet demands that he absent himself from the senses at times in order to comprehend them more fully, to return to them with a deeper appreciation of their value. The balmy, blood-heat of the south can be known only by a man who has a "mind of winter."

II

Central to any analysis of Stevens' images of northern cold is "The Snow Man" (CP, 9–10). The poet wrote that "the absence of the imagination had/ Itself to be imagined" (CP, 503), and in this poem he abstracts himself from "reality" so that he can fully appreciate its warm, natural richness. Although the poem pictures a world without humanity, a planet cleared of man's faulty conceptions, the poet in shaping his poem affirms rather than negates the human imagination, for the negative listener perceives a composite reality that is affirmative — or at least his perception is:

> For the listener, who listens in the snow,
> And, nothing himself, beholds
> Nothing that is not there and the nothing that is.

"Negation," Bergson wrote, "is only an attitude taken by the mind toward an eventual affirmation." [16] By temporarily escaping from the human condition, ignoring the fact that he is, like Yeats, "fastened to a dying animal," Stevens achieves what is probably the coldest, most naked poem in the language, a poem without hope or despair, good or evil—for all of these man-made ideas corrupt pure perception. By personifying the element of cold, Stevens attempts to make what Valéry calls "an observation with no observer." [17]

Snow, as an "objective correlative," serves Stevens well because, like the ice cream in "The Emperor of Ice-Cream" (CP, 64), it gives transience form. Just as a snowman will eventually melt, so will the poet's "mind of winter," his moment of timeless vision, be dissolved by the hot sun of the other "reality" he has only temporarily imagined away. Moreover, the snowman as a man-made image resembles a work of art, a statue, except that it claims no significance beyond the time of its life. Like man, it possesses form; like man also, it will melt back into the surrounding earth. Stevens, the romantic poet in isolation from his fellowman, seeks to create an image that will reconcile man to his own mortality and to the futility of finding any permanence uncontaminated by change. Such knowledge should not, he believes, produce despair, even when we realize the uselessness of man's creations, for man will continue to create. Crispin spends a lifetime "proving what he proves/ Is nothing . . ." (CP, 46),[18] and yet he aspires, as does the later speaker of "Like Decorations in a Nigger Cemetery" (CP, 150–58):

> Can all men, together, avenge
> One of the leaves that have fallen in autumn?
> But the wise man avenges by building his city in snow.
> (CP, 158)

Much later than "The Snow Man," when Stevens is
evolving his conception of the hero to replace the anti-
quated mythological heroes, he rejects any possibility
of representing what he has in mind by a human figure
or any artistic form because the hero "is not an Image.
It is a feeling" (CP, 278). The poet must create his myth
out of the commonplace and the ephemeral:

> Devise. Make him of mud,
> For every day. In a civiler manner,
> Devise, devise, and make him of winter's
> Iciest core, a north star, central
> In our oblivion, of summer's
> Imagination, the golden rescue . . .   (CP, 275)

   The imageless world of a snowman (who *is* the cold
that is also his "reality,") becomes the first evidence of
the positive quality that Stevens gives to "nothing"; the
poem begins an association of winter and nothingness
that will recur in the poems that follow. The visionary
state must be further purified by ridding it of any sensory
qualities, and the planet must be cleared of humanity
with all its consolatory values. It was an austerity Stevens
demanded of himself, the ascetic bread and water by
which he atoned for the hedonistic feast he made of
"reality." Without sharing Mallarmé's contempt for the
world he rejects, Stevens resembles him in the pure
state he intermittently cultivates. Mallarmé wrote: "En
vérité, je voyage, mais dans des pays inconnus et si,
pour fuir la réalité torride, je me plais à évoquer des
images froides, je te dirai que je suis depuis un mois
dans les plus purs glaciers de l'Esthétique — qu'après
avoir trouve le Néant, j'ai trouvé le Beau." [19] However,
because Stevens was never, even in his coldest poem,

able to purge himself of the love of created things, his transcendence is not mystical. He seeks no divine union; rather, he attempts to comprehend his relationship with man and his planet by assuming momentarily the non-human or metaphysical viewpoint.

A very late poem "The Course of a Particular" (OP, 96–97) displays Stevens' method. The poet confronts the "nothingness," without illusions, but we discover that, far from being nothing, the planet (and the poem) is filled with images:

> Today the leaves cry, hanging on branches swept by wind,
> Yet the nothingness of winter becomes a little less.
> It is still full of icy shades and shapen snow.

Silence is the only poem the true mystic can write, but Stevens not only speaks but also becomes the voice of a nature that cannot speak for itself. By personifying the leaves, he fills the winter void with the image of man:

> The leaves cry . . . One holds off and merely hears the cry.
> It is a busy cry, concerning someone else.
> And though one says that one is part of everything,
>
> There is a conflict, there is a resistance involved;
> And being part is an exertion that declines:
> One feels the life of that which gives life as it is.

One is both the perceiver and the perceived; one is both in the world where leaves are facts, but one is also able to "feel" the power behind facts. The poet "holds off" from actuality only so that he can hear its cry, the cry of the universal in the particular.

In the final two stanzas, Stevens negates the consoling

powers of God and man but he affirms the "cry" and "the
life of that which gives life as it is":

> The leaves cry. It is not a cry of divine attention,
> Nor the smoke-drift of puffed-out heroes, nor human cry.
> It is the cry of leaves that do not transcend themselves,
>
> In the absence of fantasia, without meaning more
> Than they are in the final finding of the ear, in the thing
> Itself, until, at last, the cry concerns no one at all.

Here is the world that "The Comedian as the Letter C"
(CP, 27–46) started with, "The world without Imagination," where one could not evade "the strict austerity/
Of one vast, subjugating, final tone" (CP, 30). Yet paradoxically, and despite Stevens' claim that the leaves
make no human cry, the poem includes the speaker
whose imagination utters the cry. As the poet himself
said, "The poem is the cry of its occasion,/ Part of the
res itself and not about it" (CP, 473). Stevens' nothingness is a positive backdrop against which man stands out
more sharply; far from a state of nonbeing, it is, what
Bergson defined, "an image full of things, an image that
includes at once that of the subject and that of the object
and, besides, a perpetual leaping from one to the other
and the refusal ever to come to rest finally on either. Evi-
dently this is not the nothing that we can oppose to
being, and put before or beneath being, for it already includes existence in general." [20] Stevens declares that
"nothingness was a nakedness, a point,/ Beyond which
fact could not progress as fact" (CP, 402), and on this
clean slate the poet creates his poetic fictions. But he
shares Sartre's belief that "we discover non-being as a
condition of a transcendence toward being." [21]
Frank Kermode in defending Stevens asserts that

"there is a poetry of the abstract," [22] and "The Snow Man" is a good example of what the poet means by that term. One of the recurring mistakes made in reading Stevens is to see him as a Platonist who, as he develops, seeks to subordinate the sensory world to the realm of pure ideas. When he says that poetry "must be abstract" he does not customarily mean philosophical abstraction, the extrapolation of idea from thing. More often he means the escape from both idea and image, the destruction of all "mind-forged manacles" in an effort to discover "the inconceivable idea of the sun" or "a heaven/ That has expelled us and our images" (CP, 381). The reader must *imagine* the nothingness that is there while the poet labors to articulate nonbeing, "as if nothingness contained a métier,/ A vital assumption, an impermanence/ In its permanent cold . . ." (CP, 526).

The difference between Stevens' use of "abstraction" and the usual philosophical one is made evident when both uses occur in another "cold" poem, and a much later one, "No Possum, No Sop, No Taters" (CP, 293–94). In a stark January scene, without sun or human warmth, the poet personifies the "broken stalks" of corn that remain after the harvest, rather than the snow. In one of his brilliant figures, the poet divorces himself from the scene, so that he can know it without the distortions of the senses:

> Snow sparkles like eyesight falling to earth,
>
> Like seeing fallen brightly away.

By clearing the scene of man, both abstract and concrete man, he is able to comprehend the nothingness articulated by the stalks:

It is in this solitude, a syllable,
Out of these gawky flitterings,

Intones its single emptiness,
The savagest hollow of winter-sound.

All of this realization of nonbeing is characteristic of
Stevens' method of abstraction, but two stanzas, by contrast, present the more conventional use of the term. The
second stanza:

The field is frozen. The leaves are dry.
Bad is final in this light.

And near the end of the poem, after the poet has trans-
ported himself from the scene:

It is here, in this bad, that we reach
The last purity of the knowledge of good.

The use of "bad" and "good," and the human values
they connote, could be seen as a defect in the poem, a
disturbing intrusion of "ideas" into the nothingness, a
descent into the value-ridden world. On the other hand,
it may be seen as the poet's attempt to project human
values upon the screen of nothingness, to see them as
real, not illusory. In either case, the poem ends with the
"abstraction blooded": evil is in the natural world and
man finds no escape from it. Man's "knowledge of good"
consists of seeing and accepting the nothingness that
Sartre and Camus came to accept in their differing ways:

The crow looks rusty as he rises up.
Bright is the malice in his eye . . .

> One joins him there for company,
> But at a distance, in another tree.

The universe is not a friendly place, neither is man able to escape its coldness by human contacts. And yet the crow's eye, like Blake's Tyger, is bright, the only thing of power in the desolate scene. Stevens is still looking, but in this later poem he is more than a man of snow who sees only nothing; he sees the malice in the crow's eye. "The Snow Man" was published in 1921; "No Possum, No Sop, No Taters" appeared in 1947. The poet's range broadens, and he introduces more personal values into the scene, but both convey a persistent Stevens' theme: Man must imagine the world without himself before he can truly know himself. Both poems aim ultimately at a clearer picture of man, not a description of nothingness or emptiness. The result of "abstraction" is not a work that exists "in the sphere of perfect uselessness," [23] but one that "helps us to live our lives" (NA, 36). The transformation of man into snow-man is momentary, and he returns with a surer knowledge of why he is *not* a snowman. As R. P. Blackmur said of Stevens: "Such a transformation amounts to an access of knowledge, as it raises to a condition where it may be rehearsed and understood in permanent form that body of emotional and sensational experience which in its natural condition makes life a torment and confusion." [24]

For Stevens, poetry can be disguise, evasion, illusion; whereas prose is the undeniable and essential body of fact to which all of us must return, if we choose honesty over self-deception. While proclaiming poetry as "the supreme fiction" necessary to help us live our lives, Stevens sometimes disparages the ultimate value of an art that is powerless before the facts of change and death.

Poetry can be a "finikin thing of air" (CP, 155) and mere "fictive flourishes" (CP, 39), but death and natural process are the profound truths. Two early poems that use the image of cold (as death) are "The Emperor of Ice-Cream" and "Cortège for Rosenbloom." In both, the bloom of life has fallen and the cold remains; both compel the reader to face death without ritual or ceremony, which, like poetry, are ultimately ineffectual; in both, the overly refined and fastidious in dress and manners is made ludicrous; both, finally, advocate an acceptance of the cold nakedness of the actual world, declaring that "the actual is a deft beneficence" (CP, 155).

The title "The Emperor of Ice-Cream" (CP, 64), like other Stevens' titles, suggests that man can assume importance by exerting a force over the transient world.[25] But because man is a part of the transience he rules, he is truly absurd. Filled with bravado, like Gulliver in Brobdingnag, he ignores his own smallness and the impossibility of achieving any lasting hold on life. Consistently, Stevens accepts rather than opposes transience; hence the most trivial and transitory thing of the world, its ice cream, can be a trope for what he has in mind. Furthermore the image reinforces his belief in "ephemeral creation." Man has a dignity of sorts: in the face of destruction he creates a realm that he can rule over. Cigars, flowers, newspapers, curds — the images of the poem evoke the impermanent and expendable; as "parts of a world" they, sadly or not, make up the whole. A line from the first stanza contains the theme of the poem: "Let be be finale of seem," which is in a way analogous to Sartre's "existence precedes essence." The facts of life — and death is one of the hardest and coldest — must be confronted without the assurances of the past or the disguises of religion or artistic creation when it assumes an ideal form beyond the world of fact. The theme is a central one in Stevens, and it was similarly phrased by Pope as "whatever is is right." [26] Both poets, different as they are, demand that man see and accept "things as they are," without probing after ultimate meaning.

The second half of the poem shows the futility of dress (artifice) in concealing the cold nakedness that lies at the center of life. The "dresser of deal" is broken; the elegant "embroidered fantails" (again suggesting human artifice, including poetry) fail to hide the cold, horny feet of reality, while the only diverting life is provided by the "muscular one" whipping his "concupiscent curds." [27] Here is the crude, physical world, divested of refined consolations, and the poet insists on seeing it: "Let the lamp affix its beam." The event is as nakedly honest as William Carlos Williams' "How to Conduct a Funeral" or "Death," poems in which he also refuses to accept any consolation from ritual:

> He's nothing at all
>   he's dead
> Shrunken up to skin
>   Put his head on
> one chair and his
> feet on another and
> he'll lie there
> like an acrobat.

In "Cortège for Rosenbloom" (CP, 79–81) nothingness is again related to cold, but in this poem the "finical carriers" who comprise the cortège are in elaborate dress and attempt, through ceremony, to give important meaning to the commonplace event of death. But although the mourners attempt to make Rosenbloom more than a

man, the "fact" of Rosenbloom's death regularly punctu-
ates, as well as opens and closes, the poem. The fancy
headdresses of the mourners cannot disguise the cold
world they move in:

> It is turbans they wear
> And boots of fur
> As they tread the boards
> In a region of frost,
> Viewing the frost.

Unconscious of reality, protected from it by their "boots
of fur," they do not return the "strictest prose" of Rosenbloom to the natural earth but carry him "into the sky"
and out of the real world. These novices of life and death
are incapable of knowing man as he is:

> It is the infants of misanthropes
> And the infants of nothingness
> That tread
> The wooden ascents
> Of the ascending of the dead.

The ritual, not the death of Rosenbloom, is "lamentable."
The noises of the cadence of the procession "jangle"
and "jumble" the "intense poem/ Of the strictest prose/
Of Rosenbloom." Far from honoring the dead, his sur-
vivors rob him of the dignity of his own death by not
recognizing that ritual is for the living and therefore
inappropriate.

   The two poems together reveal a similar attitude
toward conventional ceremony or ritual, for ceremony,
like poetry, can be an escape from reality, dress or disguise for the weak "infants" that we all are. Underneath

the poem, there is prose; underneath life, there is death. The poet celebrates the nature of things, devising his own personal incantations, but the man who dies properly is the soldier who rejects all ceremony because "religious ceremonies and delights are evasions of reality. External life, the opposite, is all a wedding with reality." [28] The soldier is honest because

> He does not become a three-days personage,
> Imposing his separation,
> Calling for pomp.
>
> Death is absolute and without memorial,
> As in a season of autumn,
> When the wind stops,
>
> When the wind stops and, over the heavens,
> The clouds go, nevertheless,
> In their direction.   (CP, 97)

A final poem, "The Man Whose Pharynx Was Bad" (CP, 96), focuses on the image of cold and is one of Stevens' most effective poems of dejection, recording the anguish of a poet in a fallow period, trapped within himself and unable to find outlet in either mind or body. A paralysis of creative will or imagination leaves him incapable of articulation: His pharynx is hopelessly bad. An uninspired Coleridge, he cannot find joy in either winter or summer, north or south:

> The time of year has grown indifferent.
> Mildew of summer and the deepening snow
> Are both alike in the routine I know.
> I am too dumbly in my being pent.

The physical abundance of summer is now "mildew,"
and winter remains inaccessible behind an "icy haze."
The quickening wind still moves, but the aeolian harp is
silent:

> The wind attendant on the solstices
> Blows on the shutters of the metropoles,
> Stirring no poet in his sleep, and tolls
> The grand ideas of the villages.

One can no longer achieve a transport through immediate
contact with the physical world because, as Stevens said,
"the sustenance of the wilderness/ Does not sustain us
in the metropoles" (CP, 142). The speaker feels that
time is out of joint, and blames the monotony of day-to-
day existence for a condition which, more correctly, is
a result of the failure of his own imaginative power:

> The malady of the quotidian. . . .
> Perhaps, if winter once could penetrate
> Through all its purples to the final slate,
> Persisting bleakly in an icy haze,
>
> One might in turn become less diffident,
> Out of such mildew plucking neater mould
> And spouting new orations of the cold.
> One might. One might. But time will not relent.

Like many of Stevens' poems, this one is about the poet
and his poetry (as he says in "The Man with the Blue
Guitar," "Poetry is the subject of the poem") or, to be
more encompassing, about human expression. The
speaker is "dumb" and cannot deliver his "orations";
undergoing a dark night of the soul, in which the comic
spirit, the buoyant humor, are absent, the poet is also

without his north and south, and the imagination which can effect the proper liaison between them.

That the poet makes time, rather than his own deficiency, the cause of his paralysis seems a futile attempt to account for the failure of creative power. (Like other romantics, Stevens is unable to explain why his powers come or go.[29] He calls one of his essays "Imagination as Value," but when the imagination fails, where is value?) Each stanza is, in fact, about time, the relentless movement of day into day ("The malady of the quotidian"), season into season ("the solstices"). For Stevens, the past is dead, the future an "airy dream," and the present moment all that he can truly know. Consequently, when the words fail to come to possess and shape the moment, the chaos, the nothingness, the cold is hardly bearable; the poet is left without a consoling sense of tradition or any hope for better times to come. Time past is time present is time future for Eliot because all times marry in mystic vision. But Stevens lives only when he can allay the relentlessness of time by language. He believes that the moment

> Itself
> Is time, apart from the past, apart
> From any future, the ever-living and being,
> The ever-breathing and moving, the constant fire.
>
> The present close, the present realized.   (CP, 238)

A poem becomes what Frost called "a momentary stay against confusion." The absence of the shaping spirit of the imagination is therefore more critical for Stevens than it is for a tradition-minded, religious poet like Eliot, who depends less on language as his final defense against the cold pressures of reality. "Our self-preservation," Stevens wrote, depends on "the sound of words" (NA, 36). Paradoxically, both Coleridge and Stevens make of their own despair a work of art whose words restore the poet to at least temporary health.

The cold is often linked in Stevens' mind with images of poverty. To be without a religious myth or the escapes of art is to face a planet that is starkly destitute, but the poet demands that man realize that he is both cold and poor. By facing and accepting the essential poverty of his condition, his own death, he can begin to create in full consciousness a liaison with his environment; as long as he denies or ignores his "iciest core" (CP, 275), he remains blissfully ignorant of his own powers and capabilities. The extraordinary man—who is not simply the poet but the man of imagination—acknowledges his poverty and thereby prevents what Collingwood calls "corruption of consciousness." [30] For example, the speaker of "Idiom of the Hero" (CP, 200–01) refuses to share the "power of positive thinking" of his society and declares, "I am the poorest of all./ I know that I cannot be mended . . . ." And when the poet devises a hero in *Notes toward a Supreme Fiction,* he will not be an Achilles, shielded by myth; he will be that destitute creature played by Charlie Chaplin:

> The man
> In that old coat, those sagging pantaloons,
>
> It is of him, ephebe, to make, to confect
> The final elegance, not to console
> Nor sanctify, but plainly to propound.   (CP, 389)

The cold and poverty, so frequently united in Stevens' poems, are not meant to be debilitating: from "winter's/

Iciest core" the imagination must create the "golden rescue"; from that man in the old coat and the sagging pantaloons the imagination must "confect/ The final elegance"; the total poverty of the snowman must awaken the imagination to an awareness of the luxury of existence.

Stevens often laments the failure of the imagination to work these changes. In the poem that immediately follows "The Snow Man" in *Harmonium,* "The Ordinary Women" (CP, 10–12), he creates people who engage poverty and cold but cannot sustain their imaginative vision. At first they are capable:

> Then from their poverty they rose,
> From dry catarrhs, and to guitars
> They flitted
> Through the palace walls.
>
> They flung monotony behind,
> Turned from their want . . .
> . . . .
> And the cold dresses that they wore,
> In the vapid haze of the window-bays,
> Were tranquil . . .

The women, like that "ordinary" evening in New Haven, are ordinary only as long as their imaginations lie fallow. Once they rise with their imaginations (symbolized here by the moonlight) they achieve an uncommon elegance:

> How explicit the coiffures became,
> The diamond point, the sapphire point,
> The sequins
> Of the civil fans!

Unfortunately, however, the vision fails and they return
to their monotonous lives. (The state in which the poet
sadly finds himself in "No Possum, No Sop, No Taters.")
The cause of the failure is never explicitly stated, but
the women's conformity and their suppressed desires
seem to weaken the power of their imaginations, their
only means of complete self-realization:

> Insinuations of desire,
> Puissant speech, alike in each,
> Cried quittance
> To the wickless halls.

Like Wordsworth and Coleridge, or Keats, Stevens describes the effects of the imagination on reality, but he
is unable to explain why the imagination comes and
goes, why its glorious light "fades into the light of common day." The escape from poverty is an act that must
be repeated continually. Although we never transcend
ourselves, except momentarily, we do return to the cold
and poverty after an imaginative flight with a *knowledge*
of our environment, "a belief in one's element" (CP,
258).

One such imaginative flight and return is described in
"Extracts from Addresses to the Academy of Fine Ideas"
(CP, 252–59) as a trip to the moon. The cold world of
inescapable fact is never denied by the "summer's
imagination"; it remains the center underneath, the
"exactest poverty":

> And then returning from the moon, if one breathed
> The cold evening, without any scent or the shade
> Of any woman, watched the thinnest light
> And the most distant, single color, about to change,

And naked of any illusion, in poverty,
In the exactest poverty, if then
One breathed the cold evening, the deepest inhalation
Would come from that return to the subtle centre.
   (CP, 258)

The center is hard to bear—one prefers summer riches
to winter poverty—and illusions are more comforting
than the vacancy they inevitably leave behind. Yet
"everything/ Falls back to coldness . . ." (CP, 147). The
weather becomes an analogue of man's inner life:

> There lies the misery, the coldest coil
> That grips the centre, the actual bite, that life
> Itself is like a poverty in the space of life,
> So that the flapping of wind around me here
> Is something in tatters that I cannot hold.
>   (CP, 298-99)

Stevens never evades looking for that "centre" or of
proclaiming its significance, for he believes that "it is
poverty's speech that seeks us out the most" (CP, 510).
In order to reach that "centre," one must be willing to
create a self "whose chiefest embracing of all wealth/ Is
poverty, whose jewel found/ At the exactest central of
the earth/ Is need" (OP, 104). The knowledge one gains
from facing that hard, cold core of poverty is similar to
Lear's tragic recognition that "unaccommodated man is
no more but such a poor, bare, forked animal," an image
reinforced by Shakespeare's fusion of images of coldness
and poverty in a single line, "Poor Tom's a-cold." Although Stevens may be a "comic spirit" (defined by
Nietzsche as that "which releases us, through art, from
the tedium of absurdity"),[31] he possesses a tragic sense
of life. The end is inherent in the beginning and, just as

in the midst of summer he imagines winter, "something
of death's poverty is heard" (CP, 477) in the midst of the
happiest perfection. Poetry itself becomes the world's
image and "When poetry is Image, life must, as Yeats
said, be tragic." [32]

The poet's need to find the language to express the
world's essential poverty is critical, because without the
act of recognition, which is the poem, the human animal
sinks into unconscious anonymity: "The soldier is poor
without the poet's lines . . ." (CP, 407). Far from writing
escapist poetry, in the usual pejorative sense of that
word, the poet must compel his audience to find "gran-
deur" not in another world but "only in misery, the af-
flatus of ruin,/ Profound poetry of the poor and of the
dead . . ." (CP, 509).[33] By expressing poverty and cold
the poem achieves tragic dimensions, not within the
literary genre called "tragedy," but within the "real"
experience that writers of tragedy only mirror.

Images of north, of a central cold and poverty, are
brought together and viewed as "tragic" in "In a Bad
Time" (CP, 426–27). The speaker realizes that the cold
"order of the northern sky" can be accepted as analogous
to the human condition only by a man who has re-
nounced, momentarily, the world's summer richness.
The man possessed of myths of his own nobility may see
but never become a part of the continuous natural
tragedy:

> But the beggar gazes on calamity
> And thereafter he belongs to it, to bread
> Hard found, and water tasting of misery.
>
> For him cold's glacial beauty is his fate.
> Without understanding, he belongs to it

> And the night, and midnight, and after, where it is.
> (CP, 426)

The bread and water come to sustain him, although they are infected by sorrow and pain. Echoing Yeats, Stevens then asks what "becomes his heart's strong core?" The answer is the strength that comes from acknowledging human mortality as inevitable and final, man's fate as unknowable: it is the strong core of a Hamlet who says, "let be."

> He has his poverty and nothing more.
> His poverty becomes his heart's strong core —
> A forgetfulness of summer at the pole.

The poem ends by evoking the muse of tragedy, but not asking that the human situation be transformed by her into *art,* and thereby made tolerable because vicariously experienced. The tragedy must be seen *in life;* therefore, he asks her to avoid the effete conventions, the trappings of tragedy (suggested by "heliotrope"):

> Speak loftier lines.
> Cry out, "I am the purple muse." Make sure
> The audience beholds you, not your gown.

Thus the poet compels the audience to see tragedy as human action, not as a literary form, Aristotle's imitation of an action. The poverty and cold must be seen behind the radiant costume of summer. (Most difficult if one lives in the perpetual summer of the south.) The world's disguises — and one of these is art — must be stripped away; and man's greatest nobility results from his power to endure barrenness, to survive the "bad time" of his

insatiable hunger for final answers. Of course, "The
greatest poverty is not to live/ In a physical world . . ."
(CP, 325). And so we endure all weathers, or as George
Herbert said in "Employment," "and so we freeze on,/
Until the grave increase our cold."

The poverty that Stevens perceives is spiritual poverty, and he believes, with Blake, that the only force
that can restore man to his lost Eden — lost through self-
negation and apathy, not through sin — is the imagination, since "God and the imagination are one . . ." (CP,
524). He feels that the "poet and painter alike live and
work in the midst of a generation that is experiencing
essential poverty in spite of fortune" (NA, 171), and that
poverty and cold must be brought to the level of consciousness before they can be mastered. The void of
Kierkegaard must be seen in anguish before it can be
leapt, but the eternal optimism of Christianity will not
do for Stevens because it denies the ultimate significance of the earth. Jung describes the world which
Stevens finds:

Just as in Christianity the vow of worldly poverty turned the
mind away from the riches of this earth, so spiritual poverty
seeks to renounce the false riches of the spirit in order to withdraw not only from the sorry remnants — which today call
themselves the Protestant church — of a great past, but also
from all the allurements of the odorous East; in order, finally,
to dwell with itself alone, where, in the cold light of consciousness, the blank barrenness of the world reaches to the very
stars.[34]

Stevens compels his readers to acknowledge such a
situation, but only as a means of discovering a cure, for
"not to have is the beginning of desire" (CP, 382). The

eternal genius of man, in the face of nothingness and eventual annihilation, without hope of heaven, creates in the poem an affirmation, a "yes," as expressed by "Esthétique du Mal" (CP, 313–26):

> How cold the vacancy
> When the phantoms are gone and the shaken realist
> First sees reality. The mortal no
> Has its emptiness and tragic expirations.
> The tragedy, however, may have begun,
> Again, in the imagination's new beginning,
> In the yes of the realist spoken because he must
> Say yes, spoken because under every no
> Lay a passion for yes that had never been broken.

The Snow Man's "mind of winter" is found to be an essential negation that clears the "basic slate" on which man can create his own images. Yeats found that the tragedies of *Hamlet* and *Lear* were affirmative and joyful, "Gaiety transfiguring all that dread," that art does not change but merely accepts and celebrates the fact that "despite every phenomenal change, life is at bottom indestructibly joyful and powerful." In the midst of poverty, Stevens praises the "Lord," but finds him contained in man's own voice which rings out and fills the void. Because "man's truth is the final resolution of everything" (NA, 175):

> Natives of poverty, children of malheur,
> The gaiety of language is our seigneur.

In one of his very late poems, "The Planet on the Table" (CP, 532–33), Stevens looks back over his lifetime production and finds satisfaction in the belief that

he has found himself and revealed—but not captured—
his world by acts of consciousness. Still committed to
"ephemeral creation," he considers his own works as he
would the leaves of autumn: "It was not important that
they survive." His only hope is that they have been
honest, true to the reality of both north and south, and
that they bear

> Some affluence, if only half-perceived,
> In the poverty of their words,
> Of the planet of which they were part.

2 SUN AND MOON

"A fluctuating between sun and moon"

*The Comedian as the
Letter C*

Stevens' use of sun and moon further reveals his constant goal: the interpenetration of imagination and reality. The poet's ambivalence, as usual, prevents us from making clear-cut equivalents for these images. The sun is an image of the thoughtless physical life, but in its life-giving power it is allied with human creativity, hence the imagination. The moon, the traditional "romantic" image of the imagination, more often suggests the weakening effects of contemplative thought, "feminine"; whereas the sun is consistently masculine. The two aspects of the poet's nature are given poetic life in the interplay of these images.

The sun as a symbol of the active virile life is celebrated in "Ploughing on Sunday" (CP, 20), a simple, unpretentious poem that seems devoid of intellectual content. That Sunday is, after all, the sun's day as well as

the Lord's is possibly the only idea implied. Returning
to language as the source of meaning, to the root of
words, Stevens creates a pagan poem of "holiday" which
defies Christian Sunday decorum. The woman in "Sunday Morning" (CP, 66–70) stayed home from church to
meditate, with the physical props of "coffee and oranges
in a sunny chair," and in the "comforts of the sun."
After her round of speculation, Stevens affirms the
power that exists, not in female introspection, but in
the Whitmanesque church of the Dionysiac physical:

> Supple and turbulent, a ring of men
> Shall chant in orgy on a summer morn
> Their boisterous devotion to the sun,
> Not as a god, but as a god might be,
> Naked among them, like a savage source.

The same "savage source" is found in "Ploughing on
Sunday." A few nouns appear in the poem, but the prec-
edence of physical activity over spiritual meditation is
achieved by an abundance of verbs in the present tense
and a participle. The tails of the birds are like the water
and wind of the exuberant day, a flurry of life. The verbs
(tosses, glitters, pours, flare, bluster, blow, spreads,
streams) envelop the speaker, who becomes a part of
his world, not alien to it:

> Remus, blow your horn!
> I'm ploughing on Sunday,
> Ploughing North America.
> Blow your horn!
>
> Tum-ti-tum,
> Ti-tum-tum-tum!
> The turkey-cock's tail
> Spreads to the sun.

The white cock's tail
Streams to the moon.
Water in the fields.
The wind pours down.

The nonsense sounds are an indication of the speaker's refusal to be governed by his rational faculties, the poet's delight in the sounds of words for themselves alone — and the range of physical affirmation reaches from sun to moon. Opposites (sun and moon) meet in the *act* of life. The poem records an experience unhampered by meaning, and explication can do little but name that experience: creative zest.

Nevertheless, "Ploughing on Sunday" is, at heart, a poem that takes on meaning when one considers the sun as a rational as well as an emotional symbol of creative power. In the introduction to his presentation of the concept of the libido, Jung says, "The sun, as Renan has observed, is the only truly 'rational' image of God, whether we adopt the standpoint of the primitive savage or of modern science." [1] It is typical of Stevens to attempt to get beyond the man-made structures of social and religious thought, back to that first idea men call God — although Stevens would object to any name that would carry with it human connotations *and* limitations. In the opening section of *Notes toward a Supreme Fiction*, for example, he discusses the sun as an idea that can be apprehended only through a rejection of stale metaphors of poetry as well as cold rational systems. The initiate must resist the temptation to depend on human analogies:

Begin, ephebe, by perceiving the idea
Of this invention, this invented world,
The inconceivable idea of the sun.

You must become an ignorant man again
And see the sun again with an ignorant eye
And see it clearly in the idea of it.   (CP, 380)

And in another poem all the "dark forms" of physical
nature, as well as human "fears of life and fears of
death," can be vanquished by the arrival of "the sun,
that brave man" (CP, 138) who cannot be reasoned into
being or explained away. He exists to dispel self-defeat-
ing, introspective thought.

Unlike Plato or Kant, Stevens strives to unite idea and
image [2] (we see the sun "*in* the idea of it"); he incorporates one in the other but refuses to call the result either
God or Phoebus because "the death of one god is the
death of all," and "Phoebus was/ A name for something
that never could be named." Man's wish to reduce all
"fictions" to himself, to limit God to his own image,
degrades and restricts the sun's force, which can remain
supreme only if it is free of man's mind. This is why the
ephebe is instructed to have an "ignorant eye," for only
by clearing the mind of preconceptions can one discover the freshness of the universe. As Stevens wrote
in "The Irrational Element in Poetry" (OP, 216–
29): "the true subject supersedes the nominal subject"
(OP, 223), and because emotions and feelings are the
source of poetry, all great poetry is irrational. We can
approach the "supreme fiction" only by means of Coleridge's "willing suspension of disbelief." No philosophy
or myth offers certain meaning for the phenomenal world:
always "The wheel [of the sun] survives its myths" and
life must survive all definitions of it.[3]

In "The Sense of the Sleight-of-Hand Man" (CP, 222),
Stevens again demands "ignorance" from the man who
would grasp life in the fullness of all its particulars.

After describing the physical scene before him, he goes beyond, to the sun:

> The fire eye in the clouds survives the gods.
> To think of a dove with an eye of grenadine
> And pines that are cornets, so it occurs,
> And a little island full of geese and stars:
> It may be that the ignorant man, alone,
> Has any chance to mate his life with life
> That is the sensual, pearly spouse, the life
> That is fluent in even the wintriest bronze.

Here the poet delights in his own metaphors because they enlarge his experience of a physical world that is, like Susanna's world in "Peter Quince at the Clavier" (CP, 89–92), "a wave, interminably flowing." The ignorant man is one who feels the sun (and the world), and allows his imagination to refresh feeling, but never strains for meaning. The only poetry, for Stevens, *finally*, is a poetry that merely celebrates existing phenomena and avoids limiting definition; it is "the fiction that results from feeling" (CP, 406).[4]

The ignorant man's desire "to mate his life with life" is Stevens' desire to merge his creative power with the sun's. In many poems the poet seeks a union of sun and self, but only occasionally is it accomplished, as in "the man-sun being hero" (CP, 280). Just as he attempts with music to unite inner and outer worlds, he uses the sun as the natural counterpart of the creative process, but there is no emblem like the blue guitar to stand between the interior and the exterior life: Only the poet himself is intermediary; alone, he must bear the heat of the sun. Stevens realized from the beginning that decay and death were integral components of reality, and like Keats he

lamented "Beauty that must die;/ And Joy, whose hand
is ever at his lips/ Bidding adieu. . . ." In "Waving Adieu,
Adieu, Adieu" (CP, 127–28), the poet accepts the inevitability of physical change and turns to the sun for consolation, asking, "What is there here but weather, what
spirit/ Have I except it comes from the sun?" The "real"
sun is not to be evaded; it is to be confronted without
disguise: [5]

> The body walks forth naked in the sun
> And, out of tenderness or grief, the sun
> Gives comfort . . .   (CP, 108)

To accept the sun as the source of all creative energy
is to humble oneself before God, if we accept Jung's contention that "the visible father, God, sun, and fire are all
mythologically synonymous." [6] Unlike Christian poets
who treat the sun as an agent of a still higher reality,
Stevens always accepts it as first cause. For Milton and
Donne, the earth is kept from annihilation (what Stevens calls "Domination of Black"), but not by the sun:
"Yet thou art rescued by a mightier fire,/ Then they old
Soule, the Sunne. . . ." [7] In Dr. Richard's terms, Donne's
Sun is the vehicle, Christ the tenor. Like the sun in Milton's "On the Morning of Christ's Nativity," it is an
"inferior flame" which is eclipsed by the Christ child:
"He saw a greater Sun appear/ Than his bright Throne,
or burning Axletree could bear." Christianity incorpo-
rated and modified the pagan symbol of the sun, but it
could never, as Stevens does, accept the pagan priority. [8]

For Stevens, human power and solar power are re-
ciprocal, even at times identical ("His self and the sun
were one . . ." [CP, 532]), and the sun is a constant reminder of his own light and warmth-giving responses
that may lie dormant under the cold winter sky.

The Sun This March

The exceeding brightness of this early sun
Makes me conceive how dark I have become,

And re-illumines things that used to turn
To gold in broadest blue, and be a part

Of a turning spirit in an earlier self.
That, too, returns from out the winter's air,

Like an hallucination come to daze
The corner of the eye. . . . (CP, 133–34)

The renewing sun operates on both inner and outer worlds and thereby parallels the imagination. Like the imagination, also, it works purposelessly, lighting the surfaces of life but never explaining itself. The word "hallucination" is significant in revealing the nature of the sun-imagination, for one of its meanings is the "experience of sensations with no external cause." It is the same sun that appears in a much later poem as "A new-colored sun, say, that will soon change forms/ And spread hallucinations on every leaf" (CP, 529). And again in "An Ordinary Evening in New Haven" (CP, 465–89), in which Stevens chooses the superiority of sun "against the lunar light" and is content to accept the fact that its influence, like man's, is limited to surfaces:

So that the approaching sun and its arrival,
Its evening feast and the following festival,

This faithfulness of reality, this mode,
This tendance and venerable holding-in
Make gay the hallucinations in surfaces. (CP, 472)

Just as the sun has within itself the power of renewal, so man possesses a psychic energy which is capable of creating him anew each day. By joining with natural process, the poet (and for Stevens "poet" usually means imaginative man) is able to find within himself the god he has been looking for externally. Upon "A Fading of the Sun" (CP, 139), people can grow "suddenly cold" and become so depressed by the idea of eventual death that their "tea is bad, bread sad." Stevens' remedy for this situation is a turning within, a rediscovery of dormant power, for, as Jung says, "to carry a god within oneself is practically the same as being God oneself": [9]

> If joy shall be without a book
> It lies, themselves within themselves,
> If they will look
> Within themselves
> And cry and cry for help?
>
> Within as pillars of the sun,
> Supports of night. The tea,
> The wine is good. The bread,
> The meat is sweet.
> And they will not die.

The only immortality man can know comes from a marriage with the god within; the mutable world then becomes hospitable because one *makes* it good. Penelope learns this in "The World as Meditation" (CP, 520–21). While she waits for an actual Ulysses to return home and fulfill her needs, she finds that her own imagination can evoke a "savage presence" which "awakens the world in which she dwells." Her desire for Ulysses becomes her desire for the sun:

> But was it Ulysses? Or was it only the warmth
>   of the sun
> On her pillow? The thought kept beating in
>   her like her heart.
> The two kept beating together. It was
>   only day.

The interior sun (the libido) merges with the sun out-side and Penelope realizes that "the barbarous strength within her [can] never fail." [10] She apprehends that life is "becoming" and that as a part of what Stevens feels is "an always incipient cosmos . . ." (OP, 115) she can never die.

"The Comedian as the Letter C" is one of the first poems in which the sun-moon antithesis is developed in any systematic way, and it seems clear that these images enlarge the north-south polarity discussed ear-lier. Stevens was never happy paying the price that the poem demands: detachment (even when temporary, as on the blue guitar) from the reality which is the source of its being. He pictures the complete man as one who can find satisfaction in life, without the necessity of ex-plaining it; [11] however, he was never able to desert his cold north where the imagination was "cold in a boreal mistiness of the moon" (CP, 34). He realized his limita-tion when he wrote in "Two or Three Ideas" (OP, 210–16): "The trouble is . . . that men in general do not create in light and warmth alone. They create in dark-ness and coldness" (OP, 210). Although the sun is pre-dominately Stevens' image of creative power,[12] the moon can provide reflective power which at its best can affirm the sun's existence.

The moon, as numerous critics have noted, is one of Stevens' symbols for the imagination, but it is an inconsistent symbol,[13] and many times in the "Comedian as the Letter C" it suggests self-indulgent make-believe, rather than the authentic, primary power of the sun. The imagination separated from the concrete reality which it reveals becomes weak, anemic, "more mist than moon." Crispin tries to find his reason-for-being in the lifeless cold of "mental moonlight":

> Perhaps the Arctic moonlight really gave
> The liaison, the blissful liaison,
> Between himself and his environment . . .   (CP, 34)

But before we are far along in his quest for identity — and for a poetic — he realizes that total devotion to the moon can be a sign of feminine weakness:

> It seemed
> Illusive, faint, more mist than moon, perverse,
> Wrong as a divagation to Peking,
> To him that postulated as his theme
> The vulgar, as his theme and hymn and flight,
> A passionately niggling nightingale.
> Moonlight was an evasion or, if not,
> A minor meeting, facile, delicate.   (CP, 34–35)

Crispin's association of moonlight with the nightingale indicates Stevens' distrust of outmoded images, no longer capable of expressing a present reality. Just as the poet rejects traditional religious myths, so he feels compelled to purge even his own personal symbols of sun and moon of their past life and conventional associations. The nightingale as a "poetic" image is one with the past, and Crispin, like the speaker of "Autumn Refrain" (CP, 160), resents "the yellow moon of words about the nightingale" and welcomes the noise of pres-

ent day which "grates these evasions of the nightingale . . . ." The moon must be stripped of all its romantic
trappings [14] and seen, like the sun, "in the idea of it," or
seen like the moon in "The Man on the Dump" (CP,
201–03):

> Everything is shed; and the moon comes up as
>   the moon
> (All its images are in the dump) and you see
> As a man (not like an image of a man),
> You see the moon rise in the empty sky.

Crispin, however, finds that he is unable to divorce
himself from the weaknesses of his time. When he goes
through his artistic rite of passage, until "nothing of
himself/ Remained," he still cannot see the sun for what
it is: his powerful libido that can be willed toward productive ends. He cannot comprehend it because his
"moon" sensibility evokes a feminine context for the
masculine sun:

> the sun
> Was not the sun because it never shone
> With bland complaisance on pale parasols,
> Beetled, in chapels, on the chaste bouquets.   (CP, 29)

"Parasols" are consistently used by Stevens to designate
fancy rather than imagination, feminine artifice rather
than virile art. Because they help people to evade the
full force of the sun, they serve as a perfect image to
reveal Crispin's weakness at this point in the poem. He
is still not ready for a raw confrontation with either
reality or the self. He is like the speaker in "Certain
Phenomena of Sound" (CP, 286–87) who "opened wide/

A parasol, which I had found, against/ The sun." It is
only later in the poem that Crispin accepts his duality
(including his masculine and feminine natures) [15] and
makes what is probably the clearest statement of Stevens' conception of the relation of sun and moon. Neither, he finds, can be the image of the consummate existence; both are essential to an understanding of "things
as they are," just as a woman and a man are essential to
procreation:

> Thus he conceived his voyaging to be
> An up and down between two elements,
> A fluctuating between sun and moon,
> A sally into gold and crimson forms,
> As on this voyage, out of goblinry,
> And then retirement like a turning back
> And sinking down to the indulgences
> That in the moonlight have their habitude.   (CP, 35)

Although Stevens' idea of perfection would be "the com-
mingling of sun and moon" (OP, 50), he finds that the
"fluctuation between sun and moon" comes closer to an
accurate representation of man's role within natural
process.[16] The "retirement" or "indulgences" afforded
by the moon suggest escape and self-indulgence; and
yet the moon provides the isolation and calm required
for artistic labor, the peace that counters the warring
elements of life. Crispin's imaginative and emotional
conflicts, his "fluctuation between sun and moon," is
paralleled in the rhythm of nature: summer followed by
winter, day followed by night. Moreover, the artist's interior battle is but a variation of the literal wars taking
place in the external world. The conclusion of the later
Notes toward a Supreme Fiction demonstrates this universal "fluctuation":

> Soldier, there is a war between the mind
> And sky, between thought and day and night. It is
> For that the poet is always in the sun,
>
> Patches the moon together in his room
> To his Virgilian cadences, up down,
> Up down. It is a war that never ends.
>
> Yet it depends on yours. The two are one.
>   (CP, 407)

Just as the imagination depends on reality for its life, so is the poet involved in mankind: he suffers to articulate its suffering.

Stevens' affinity for the sun and his distrust of the moon may be supported further, I believe, by the fact that sun appears over twice as many times in the total work as does moon.[17] Moreover, despite the traditional association of moon and imagination, the poet often tends to employ adjectives that emphasize its deceptive or illusory nature, its "pale coherences," its "shadowless" realm, and the poet always welcomes the morning which "throws off stale moonlight and shabby sleep" (CP, 382). Stevens avoids a total commitment to the female imagination. Always returning to masculine fact, he is unlike Mallarmé, who courted the moon's favor almost to the exclusion of the waking world: "to *name* an object is to suppress three-quarters of the enjoyment of a poem, which is made up of gradual guessing; the dream is to suggest it." [18] Stevens shared Mallarmé's distrust of naming, but he could never sever completely his relationship with fact, what he calls the "essential prose." The moon often signifies an escape from a world of process, but it is finally in change that Stevens finds his "meaning," which

resides
In a permanence composed of impermanence,
A faithfulness as against the lunar light . . .   (CP, 472)

The world's pattern, its "beauty," is "fatal in the moon" (CP, 472) but "in the flesh it is immortal" (CP, 91). The sun's arrival each day makes us happy with wakeful surfaces. A commitment to the moon entails isolation and cold, both of which Stevens confronts in order to overcome. The sun rescues man from the formless depths of the unconscious.

In "Mrs. Alfred Uruguay" (CP, 248–49) the hero of the poem is not the elegant Mrs. Uruguay, whose addiction to the make-believe of moonlight is never quite cured; he is the "rider intent on the sun," the virile poet who, though conscious of his own poverty—he is "no chevalere and poorly dressed"—is capable of using his imagination to create the world anew, to turn his poverty into riches. That "moonlight" suggests a delusive light rather than the true light of the imagination is made clear by the woman's attempt to "wipe away moonlight like mud." She desires to climb to the "real," but her despairing attitude prevents her from discovering a "capable imagination." Her moonlight, like her velvet, is superficial, and they both disguise naked reality. Although she labors to create a new self, her selfish rejection of the world and of possibility leaves her destitute: "To be, regardless of velvet, could never be more/ Than to be, she could never differently be,/ Her no and no made yes impossible." [19]

That man is equated with sun and woman with moon is plain: As the sun goes down, the hero descends the mountain; as the moon rises, the woman climbs. Having experienced the real sun (of extraversion) the man can now turn within himself for the "ultimate elegance: the imagined land." Natural changes are paralleled by psychic changes.[20] For the woman, however, who exists only in the frail "brown blues of evening" and the illusive light of the moon, the world is a surrealistic scene in which "the moonlight crumbled to degenerate forms . . . ." We find that the poem presents a central Stevens' theme: that life's fiction (moon) cannot be divorced from the actual world (sun), which is the source of its power and light.

Because of Stevens' ambivalent handling of moon images, Michel Benamou in his praiseworthy essay comparing Stevens and the Symbolist poets is misleading when he states: "All but six poems of *Harmonium* exemplify the maternal role of the imagination," whereas only six poems "announce the sun-style to come."[21] In an appendix to "Wallace Stevens and The Symbolist Imagination," Benamou lists thirty uses of sun and forty-four of moon in *Harmonium* (he includes "moonlight" in his count) but he fails to point out that the moon is not, for the most part, employed *affirmatively* as a symbol for the imagination. "The night is hostile," he writes, "and imagination safeguards us. The moon is one of its inventions."[22] But as early as *Harmonium* Stevens had evolved his conception of the alternating current between sun and moon. "Lunar Paraphrase" (CP, 107), which Benamou feels illustrates the imagination at work, suggests withdrawal and passivity more than active imaginative power.

Lunar Paraphrase

The moon is the mother of pathos and pity.

When, at the wearier end of November,
Her old light moves along the branches,
Feebly, slowly, depending upon them;

When the body of Jesus hangs in a pallor,
Humanly near, and the figure of Mary,
Touched on by hoar-frost, shrinks in a shelter
Made by the leaves, that have rotted and fallen;
When over the houses, a golden illusion
Brings back an earlier season of quiet
And quieting dreams in the sleepers in darkness —

The moon is the mother of pathos and pity.

The season of decay is matched by a light that is old and feeble; the whole poem suggests cold, decay, escape into dream. It is fitting that Stevens should associate the myth of Christianity with the "golden illusion" of the moon, since for him the myth, like the romantic nightingale, cannot exist in the full light of consciousness.[23] The moon "pallor" of Christ, the "hoar-frost" that surrounds Mary do not declare a viable myth; neither does the "pity" of the archetype do more than soften the reality that Stevens celebrates in other poems. The moonlight of "Lunar Paraphrase" resembles the "moonlight on the thick, cadaverous bloom/ That Yuccas breed . . ." (CP, 31) — the ghastly white blossoms that Crispin in "The Comedian as the Letter C" must *make the most of.*

The moon is linked with night and obscurity (it is an "obscure moon lighting an obscure world . . ." [CP, 288]) and a continual temptation to the poet who could easily surrender to a less painful state. All of the Ancient Mariner's punishments, as Kenneth Burke has pointed out, were suffered "under the aegis of the sun" and his "cure was effected under the aegis of the moon." [24] The identity which the Mariner finally achieves is a result of an awareness of the dual nature of the force active in the universe; he realizes that although the sun is "like God's own head" (the wrathful God of the Old Testament) there is an ameliorating force which, like the New Testament Christ, offers feminine compassion, the moon, "the mother of pathos and pity."

In "The Motive for Metaphor" (CP, 288) the poet, contrary to Roy Harvey Pearce's general contention, is not avoiding the sun; he is looking at his own weakness objectively and is, indirectly, questioning the evasions signified by both "moon" and "metaphor." By employing "you" instead of "I" Stevens is able to consider an essentially psychical problem. The poet is critical of the man who prefers the half-realized state of autumn, when "the wind moves like a cripple among the leaves . . . ," and the spring, "with the half colors of quarter-things . . . ." The moon's obscurity, accompanying the meaningless changes of the seasons, is the motive for the poet's poems, which attempt to penetrate that obscurity. But admirable as this cause is, Stevens is again not happy with the cost of creation: loss of intimate contact with the actual sun. He laments his

> shrinking from
> The weight of primary noon,
> The A B C of being,
>
> The ruddy temper, the hammer
> Of red and blue, the hard sound—
> Steel against intimation—the sharp flash,
> The vital, arrogant, fatal, dominant X.

The masculine assertion of the last line is what Stevens favors over the passive life led under the moon. Rather than the half-colors of the moon, here is the ruddy temper of the sun; rather than soft feminine "melting clouds" here is the weight of primary noon. Reality is hard steel, not the gossamer disguises of metaphor.

Fearing the moon-mawkishness and effeminacy that characterize romantic poetry at its worst, Stevens would reject Keats's attempt in *Endymion* to transform the moon into Phoebe, Selena, Artemis, Diana, or Cynthia, goddesses by whom the poet hopes to escape from his consciousness of human limitations. When Keats, in dream, sees the moon it is a poetic *idea,* and the impoverished earth has no symbol capable of representing it:

> Speak, stubborn earth, and tell me where, O where
> Hast thou a symbol of her golden hair?
> Not oat-sheaves drooping in the western sun . . .[25]

The season of decay ruled by "the maturing sun" eventually becomes the reality accepted by Keats ("To Autumn"), but in *Endymion* the poet is still trying to find an image capable of representing ideal permanence. The moon is a source of trouble for Stevens because his conscious mind resents any identification with the subconscious or anima.[26] The "virile" poet often distrusts the means of his own creativity when it involves concessions to the feminine moon, who encourages introspection and self-delusion. Stevens would probably agree with Yeats "that Blake, who for all his protest was glad to be alive, and ever spoke of his gladness, would have worshipped in some chapel of the Sun, but that Shelley, who hated life because he sought 'more in life than any understood,' would have wandered, lost in a ceaseless reverie, in some chapel of the star of infinite desire." [27]

The need to share the warmth of the sun with other

people and at the same time to be able to achieve the cold detachment necessary for art creates the frustration that underlies the improvisations of "The Man With the Blue Guitar" (CP, 165–84). Sections VII and VIII reveal a moon that is La Mer, "the merciful good," but also the moon whose tides (of the unconscious) withdraw the poet from humanity.

> It is the sun that shares our works.
> The moon shares nothing. It is a sea.
>
> When shall I come to say of the sun,
> It is a sea; it shares nothing;
>
> The sun no longer shares our works
> And the earth is alive with creeping men,
>
> Mechanical beetles never quite warm?
> And shall I then stand in the sun, as now
>
> I stand in the moon, and call it good,
> The immaculate, the merciful good,
>
> Detached from us, from things as they are?
> Not to be part of the sun? To stand
>
> Remote and call it merciful?
> The strings are cold on the blue guitar.
>   (CP, 168)

We saw in "Lunar Paraphrase," that the moon's "golden illusion" seems to bring a loss of consciousness rather than vivid creativity. Devotion to the moon entails isolation, and yet out of this "sea" must rise the consciousness that the poet provides for his community. After a night of chaos and storm comes

The vivid, florid, turgid sky,
The drenching thunder rolling by,

The morning deluged still by night,
The clouds tumultuously bright

And the feeling heavy in cold chords
Struggling toward impassioned choirs . . .
(CP, 169)

The poet struggles to free himself from his own "cold chords" and join the "choirs" of men-in-association, just as the sun labors to bring warmth to the earth. The sun and the poet's imagination are only denied to the "mechanical beetles" whose ignorance (both in the sense of denial and lack of awareness) divorces them from "natural" feeling. Stevens sees the artist as one who, through conflict with the sea, his devotion to the sun, restores men to a consciousness of their own innate powers but offers no cure-all for their anxieties. As Collingwood says, "For the evils which come from that ignorance the poet as prophet suggests no remedy, because he has already given one. The remedy is the poem itself. Art is the community's medicine for the worst disease of mind, the corruption of consciousness." [28]

The artist's duty to awaken society from its euphoria overrides Stevens' instinctual attraction to the private satisfactions offered by the moon.[29] The world of moonlight described in "Academic Discourse at Havana" (CP, 142–45) is appealingly soft and colorless, but it exists to be opposed:

The moonlight is not yellow but a white
That silences the ever-faithful town.

How pale and how possessed a night it is,
How full of exhalations of the sea . . .
All this is older than its oldest hymn,
Has no more meaning than tomorrow's bread.
But let the poet on his balcony
Speak and the sleepers in their sleep shall move,
Waken, and watch the moonlight on their floors.

The moon's absence of color, its pallor and its silence, can annihilate human achievement and win men back to what W. H. Auden describes as a "state of barbaric vagueness and disorder out of which civilisation has emerged and into which, unless saved by the efforts of gods and men, it is always liable to relapse."[30] Stevens' use of "but" is noteworthy because one would expect what follows to supply the missing "meaning." However, the poet's voice does not explain experience, it merely makes us aware of its quality. The sleepers *move* and *wake* and *watch*, but they do not rationally *know*. A true poet should try to incorporate sun and moon, be conscious while in the midst of generative sleep.

Another poem that focuses on images of sun and moon is "A Rabbit as King of the Ghosts" (CP, 209). The theme of the poem might well be: How the imagination can transform the world into an image that eliminates man's fear of any power beyond himself. But such a statement is questionable because of the fact that Stevens can use both sun and moon as images of the imagination. The rabbit, out of the sun, is able to think away his antagonist, the cat, and make the world *his* world, "the cat forgotten in the moon." The poem would seem to be evidence of Stevens' rejection of all mindless people who make of the moon "their own attendant ghosts" (CP, 137), and whose illusions keep them from a knowledge of the actual world. Daniel Fuchs' clear analysis of the poem supports this Stevens' pattern,[31] but there could be another reading, equally consistent. Although the rabbit evades the sun of raw reality and full consciousness ("fat cat, red tongue, green mind, white milk . . ."), he is able to imagine, like the poet, a "supreme fiction" which helps him to live his life. The poor rabbit is guilty of "evading the pressure of reality," but in so doing does he not perform the role Stevens defines for the poet? In "The Noble Rider and the Sound of Words," Stevens writes: "The mind has added nothing to human nature. It is a violence from within that protects us from a violence without. It is the imagination pressing back against the pressure of reality. It seems, in the last analysis, to have something to do with our self-preservation . . ." (NA, 36). For the moment of the imaginative act, at least, the rabbit is able to effect an armistice with the fearsome cat.

Equating rabbit with man and cat with reality is certainly a possible scheme. The terrible actuality of the world, the inevitability of mortality, is what exists and cannot be rationalized away; neither can it be made tolerable by systems of religion or philosophy. As a humanist, Stevens sees man as compelled to create a myth of self by which he can make external nature tolerable — but without the aid of tradition. ("Sunday Morning" is a case in point.) Once the rabbit has tranquilized his conceptual mind, he is able to experience, with the aid of the imagination, a harmony with his surroundings:

> Then there is nothing to think of. It comes of itself;
> And east rushes west and west rushes down,
> No matter. The grass is full

> And full of yourself. The trees around are for you,
> The whole of the wideness of night is for you,
> A self that touches all edges,
>
> You become a self that fills the four corners
>   of night.

The theme—the power of the human imagination to order external nature—is hardly disguised by the animal fable. The rabbit is not unlike the woman in "The Idea of Order at Key West" (CP, 128–30).

> She was the single artificer of the world
> In which she sang. And when she sang, the sea,
> Whatever self it had, became the self
> That was her song, for she was the maker . . .

Despite the rabbit's weak evasions, he is able to reduce the "fat cat" to a "little green cat" and finally to "a bug in the grass." In a similar way, the incomprehensible and antagonistic force of reality is reduced to human terms by the poet. Stevens' unfixed attitude toward sun and moon is nowhere more obvious: The moon suggests a distortion of the real world, an evasion, or an escape from consciousness; but it also fosters the creative imagination which can bring order out of the chaos of reality and a new enlargement of consciousness.

In general, however, Stevens would like to experience reality directly "with the sight/ Of simply seeing, without reflection." Only by contrast can the rabbit's moonlight creation in "A Rabbit as King of the Ghosts" be looked on in a favorable way. A limited moon-existence would deny Stevens the direct confrontation he desires; in fact, a life lived within the confines of the moon would

be monotonous, the environment of the unchanging
mind. The sun, in contrast, promises freedom within
the certainty of change. Reality, as the poet says in "An
Ordinary Evening in New Haven":

> is fatal in the moon and empty there.
> But, here, allons. The enigmatical
> Beauty of each beautiful enigma
>
> Becomes amassed in a total double-thing.
> We do not know what is real and what is not.
> We say of the moon, it is haunted by the man
>
> Of bronze whose mind was made up and who,
>   therefore, died.
> We are not men of bronze and we are not dead.
> His spirit is imprisoned in constant change.
>
> But ours is not imprisoned. It resides
> In a permanence composed of impermanence,
> In a faithfulness as against the lunar light . . .
>   (CP, 472)

The moon is linked with the statue, the man of bronze
which, as we shall later see, Stevens often employs as
the image of dead form. The moon here offers imprison-
ment rather than the freedom Dostoyevsky found in the
"incessant process of achievement." Whereas Yeats
finds both moon and bronze images congenial to his
vision, Stevens is in general uneasy with their connotations.

In "Byzantium" Yeats envisions a moon-existence, a
consummate sensuous state in which one escapes "the
fury and the mire of human veins." Unlike the later
poems, in which he sadly accepts "the foul rag-and-bone

shop of the heart," in "Byzantium" he imagines the possibility of transcending the world, together with its fitful changes:

> The unpurged images of day recede;
> The Emperor's drunken soldiery are abed;
> Night resonance recedes, night-walker's song
> After great cathedral gong;
> A starlit or a moonlit dome disdains
> All that man is,
> All mere complexities,
> The fury and the mire of human veins.

The world must *recede* and its solar people (the Emperor's drunken soldiery) must be deadened before the superhuman image can be revealed. The Emperor's ideal flame can be approached only at midnight, and the miraculous bird "in glory of changeless metal" cannot exist under the changing light of the sun. Yeats's moonlit realm is the permanence that Stevens considers but finally rejects because of its static quality. For Yeats, however, Phase Fifteen of the Moon, which "Byzantium" dramatizes, is a longed-for phase of "complete beauty":

As all effort has ceased, all thought has become image, because no thought could exist if it were not carried toward its own extinction, amid fear or in contemplation; and every image is separate from every other, for if image were linked to image, the soul would awake from its immovable trance.[32]

Whereas Yeats passionately yearns for transcendence, Stevens merely entertains the possibility of transcendence in order to affirm the concrete. In the flame of Byzantium, image has been absorbed by idea so that it is a "flame that cannot singe a sleeve." The physical limitation of images has, like the images themselves, receded—in this ideal phase of the moon. But for Stevens, those who attempt to get beyond—rather than *through*—the world are doomed to failure. In "How to Live. What to Do" (CP, 125–26), the couple at night, under cover of the moon, feeling the cold winds, try to get beyond the physical sun to discover its platonic idea:

> They that had left the flame-freaked sun
> To seek a sun of fuller fire.

They are faced, however, by a rock barrier which, like the mask Ahab tries to penetrate, prevents them from knowing whether a purified fire exists. Stevens' world remains "unpurged" and the couple accept their failure, content with the sounds of the *real* wind "joyous and jubilant and sure." The only permanence or certainty that Stevens finds is in the image of the changing wind. The sun is seen again as being-without-cause, like the irrational human creativity which it so often symbolizes.

Stevens employs the candle as a variant of the sun image. In both of his early plays, *Three Travelers Watch a Sunrise* (OP, 127–43) and *Carlos Among the Candles* (OP, 144–50) the sun-candle is the light of the imagination, which reveals reality. In the first, the three travelers seek seclusion from the "poverty" of the human condition, hoping to find in isolation a state of pure being similar to that of the sun, "like the seclusion of sunrise/ Before it shines on any house." To these aesthetic misanthropes, the world seems like porcelain, and they hope to escape human involvement by making the world into an artifact like Keats's urn:

> There is a seclusion of porcelain
> That humanity never invades.

Removed from social contact, stationary in "windless pavilions" of the mind (wind is one of Stevens' obsessive images of natural change), one traveler equates a candle with the sun, illustrating how the sun — and man's imagination — creates the world it lives in. Another comments that the candle, like poetry, exists for itself alone, with no utilitarian value: "And shines, perhaps, for the beauty of shining." [33] Here Stevens is courting pure poetry, tempted by an art without a social context. However, even in these early works Stevens never accepts an aesthetic involving transcendence. He always returns to the human condition (involving as it does his concept of "poverty"), despite his dissatisfaction, at times, with its crude uncertainties:

> When the court knew beauty only,
> And in seclusion,
> It had neither love nor wisdom.
> These came through poverty
> And wretchedness,
> Through suffering and pity.
> It is the invasion of humanity
> That counts.

Involvement with humanity gives significance to being, because "nothing is beautiful/ Except with reference to ourselves . . .". As the sun rises, a girl arrives, bringing news of personal tragedy, and the risen sun reveals death and anguish as well as love "painted on this porcelain." Just as the suns come perpetually, one following another, so does man succeed man and "one candle re-

places/ Another." Both the sun and "the candle of the
sun" (the imagination) are means of rescuing humanity
from the "domination of black," the blackness of isolation. The figures come seeking loss of self, but they
finally cannot ignore the inner and outer lights which
become one, so that

> Sunrise is multiplied,
> Like the earth on which it shines,
> By the eyes that open on it . . .

The sun and the candle both create the world anew, both
illuminate and quicken static form.[34]

The second play, *Carlos Among the Candles*, is a
monologue-ballet in which an "eccentric pedant of
about forty" (who resembles the speaker of "Le Monocle
de Mon Oncle") also confronts the problem choice between isolation and social involvement. The thoughtful
Carlos enjoys the pleasure of being the single candle in
a world of darkness, whose solitude, he says, "becomes
my own. I become a part of the solitude of the candle."
As he lights a series of candles, he introduces the idea
of man-in-association, "other people," and finds that
"the pulse of the crowd will beat out the shallow pulses
. . . it will fill me." The wind, the external fact which
outlasts all introspection, however, suddenly extin-
guishes several candles, and the hero, dismayed by the
subordination of the human to the natural world, tries
by a sequence of imaginative leaps and inventions,
analogies and similes, to fix *in the mind* the remaining
candles which must be put out. But after all lights are
gone, the door is opened on external nature, and the
play ends with the hero joyfully accepting a world he
could not imagine away: "Oh, ho! Here is matter beyond

invention." Even at this early date Stevens will not allow his love for the imagination to lure him away from the physical world as the ultimate end of knowledge. The distinction between inventing and discovering, as we shall see, was important to him. The inventions of the imagination are too often "false engagements of the mind" rather than insights into reality. Proust's biographer has, I believe, clarified Stevens' distinction:

in *A la Recherche,* and perhaps in all great works of art, the true function of the imagination is, paradoxically, not to imagine — in the sense of inventing or transforming — but to see: to see the reality which is concealed by habit and the phenomenal world.[35]

The equation that the Chinese in *Three Travelers Watch a Sunrise* make between the sun and a candle ("This candle is the sun" [OP, 130]) is continued with variations in other poems. Thus a candle becomes the illuminating power of the creative artist[36] in "Valley Candle" (CP, 51):

> My candle burned alone in an immense valley.
> Beams of the huge night converged upon it,
> Until the wind blew.
> Then beams of the huge night
> Converged upon its image,
> Until the wind blew.

The converging darkness and the disorder of the wind are like the "wilderness" that defines the jar in "Anecdote of the Jar" (CP, 76). But the force also reaches out to negate human achievement. The "image" of the phenomenal world remains fixed in the mind after the actual candle is extinguished, but in the end it is the

wind, symbol of change and flux, that directs all.[37] The
darkness is "essential" because without it the light is
purely of the mind, a frail illusion. With it, a single individual is large against space:

> One says a German chandelier—
> A candle is enough to light the world.
>
> It makes it clear. Even at noon
> It glistens in essential dark.   (CP, 172)

The candle may represent a "saint" (CP, 223) whose
individual existence gives intensity to life, but even this
image remains a part of "essential shadow" which can
never be ignored or clarified. Man may through his
imagination loom "large against space" (CP, 245), but
the space is a necessary backdrop on which his light is
projected. Unlike symbolist poets who attempt to transcend the phenomenal world, Stevens accepts the comforts and warmth of light while acknowledging the cold
and darkness they play upon. The symbolists, so heavily
indebted to Plato, continued rather than opposed a tradition—and the tradition was idealism. For most symbolists, the only reality is supernal.

Two late poems of Stevens, existing side by side in
the *Collected Poems,* reveal in their use of the candle
image how the poet differs from the French Symbolists
in his relationship to the physical world. In "A Quiet
Normal Life" (CP, 523) a man existing in shadow and
cold has a candle "so barely lit." He does not reject the
world or attempt to transcend it; he accepts

> a world in which, like snow,
> He became an inhabitant, obedient
> To gallant notions on the part of cold.

He is also obedient to "gallant notions on the part of night," for both make him acutely aware of the "crickets' chords" outside, the sound of a world of change that can never be clarified by the mind's candlelight, only experienced as phenomenal sound. The poem ends:

> There was no fury in transcendent forms.
> But his actual candle blazed with artifice.

The imagination can heighten the actual candle, but the "idea" of the candle (Plato's "transcendent forms") is lifeless because it is separated from life and, as Stevens says in one of his *Adagia:* "To be at the end of fact is not to be at the beginning of imagination but it is to be at the end of both" (OP, 175).

The second poem, "Final Soliloquy of the Interior Paramour" (CP, 524), indicates by its title that the power for lighting the darkness must come from within man himself who cannot, as Coleridge said in "Dejection: an Ode," "hope from outward forms to win/ The passion and the life, whose fountains are within." All the myths have lost their "fury" and the speaker finds consolation in the world around him, which in his need he half-creates:

> Within a single thing, a single shawl
> Wrapped tightly round us, since we are poor,
>   a warmth,
> A light, a power, the miraculous influence.

Stevens accepts the "obscurity of an order," and has faith in the power that "arranged the rendezvous" of life. Men, he feels, cannot find final answers, but nevertheless

> We say God and the imagination are one . . .
> How high that highest candle lights the dark.
>
> Out of this same light, out of the central mind,
> We make a dwelling in the evening air,
> In which being there together is enough.

Stevens accepts the productive obscurity and does not yearn nostalgically for a lost faith. By equating God with the imagination, he makes a "dwelling" and his love becomes not a recompense or consolation but a fulfillment, his "interior paramour" lighting his world. His faith is a faith in himself.[38]

Stevens found that the candle was a happier choice of an image to continue his sun symbolism. With its self-generating light which overcomes the darkness, the candle is appropriate as the solitary male principle, the imagination creating forms on the dark walls of mother earth. Stevens not only made the candle an extension of the sun ("The candle of the sun" [OP, 142]), but with it he also achieved one of the identities he labored for ("The candle is the sun" [OP, 130]). Although his use of the image was limited, it nevertheless focused both of his early plays and appeared significantly in one of his best late poems, "To an Old Philosopher in Rome" (CP, 508–11).

The candle in this poem "evades the sight" as it strives toward transcendence, suggesting that the philosopher seeks to find that which is "beyond the eye," beyond the "horizons of perception":

> A light on the candle tearing against the wick
> To join a hovering excellence, to escape
> From fire and be part only of that of which
>
> Fire is the symbol: the celestial possible.

But for Stevens, as for Santayana, the celestial possible must be "realized" only in human terms, "So that we feel, in this illumined large,/ The veritable small . . . ." Finally, man cannot transcend himself, and just as the philosopher "stops upon this threshold" so the poet must stop before the ineffable and be content with the actual candle, "the design of all his words":

> It is a kind of total grandeur at the end,
> With every visible thing enlarged and yet
> No more than a bed, a chair and moving nuns,
> The immensest theatre, the pillared porch,
> The book and candle in your ambered room.

3 MUSIC AND THE SEA

> "Some harmonious skeptic soon in a
>   skeptical music
> Will unite these figures of men and
>   their shapes
> Will glisten again with motion, the
>   music
> Will be motion and full of shadows."
>
> *Sad Strains of a Gay Waltz*

One of Wallace Stevens' affinities with the Symbolist poets is his fascination with music and its power of imposing form upon the chaos or flux of human experience, as well as upon the disorder of external nature. "What was baptized *Symbolism*," wrote Valéry, "can be very simply described as the common intention of several groups of poets (otherwise mutually inimical) to 're-claim their own from music.' The secret of the movement is nothing else." [1] Stevens' choice of the harmonium to serve as emblem for his first gathering of poems and his use of the guitar as a symbol of the poetic or imaginative act reveal a deep concern with images of music that persists throughout his work. In "Of Modern Poetry" (CP, 239–40), he found himself best identified, not as a scholar—although "poetry is the scholar's art" (OP, 167) —or a rabbi,[2] a philosopher, or a metaphysician, but as:

> A metaphysician *in the dark,* twanging
> An instrument, twanging a wiry string that gives
> Sounds passing through sudden rightnesses, wholly
> Containing the mind, below which it cannot descend,
> Beyond which it has no will to rise.   (CP, 240)[3]
>   [My italics]

That the poet finds his unique expression in sounds rather than ideas is what distinguishes his "act of the mind" from that of workers in other disciplines. The poet never reasons himself out of his darkness; he accepts obscurity as the inescapable and necessary background for his compositions, "at the sound/ Of which, an invisible audience listens,/ Not to the play, but to itself . . .". These sounds are what tame the giant of reality in "The Plot against the Giant" (CP, 6–7). The three girls are, in effect, artists, and poetry is the plot that will ultimately undo "the chaos and barbarism of reality."[4] The yokel comes "maundering," which suggests both languid movement and lack of articulation, muttering. Each girl uses imagery as her defense against the monster: the first employs "odors"; the second, "colors"; but it is the third who, like Ariel,[5] defeats her Caliban with musical sounds:

> Oh, la . . . le pauvre!
> I shall run before him,
> With a curious puffing.
> He will bend his ear then.
> I shall whisper
> Heavenly labials in a world of gutterals.
> It will undo him.

Because reality for Stevens can be "chaos and barbarism," he frequently employs the image of the sea to

represent that formless mass on which order must be
imposed. Like Cuchulain, Stevens fights the sea, but his
weapon is music. The poet's first full representation of
the poet as musician dealing with the sea of reality occurs in "The Comedian as the Letter C."

Crispin is both a "musician of pears" and a "lutanist
of fleas," a musician or poet manqué who through his
encounter with the sea enlarges his awareness of himself and his world. At first he is hopelessly dominated
by the reality he wishes to control. With his "baton"
(Prospero's art), his only device for directing the sea,
the comedian seems ridiculous. He hopes to evolve a
new "self" but his raw material seems too raw:

> The whole of life that still remained in him
> Dwindled to one sound strumming in his ear,
> Ubiquitous concussion, slap and sigh,
> Polyphony beyond his baton's thrust.   (CP, 28)

The sea is, of course, both the external and the internal
chaos [6] that man perpetually hopes to shape, and even
though Crispin is "merest miniscule" he, like Stevens,
does not advocate an escapist, art-for-art's-sake credo.
He wishes to harmonize the world of mind with the
phenomenal world, but he refuses to be satisfied with
a diverting music which refines away "the storm" and
"the wind,/ Tempestuous clarion . . ." (CP, 32). He must
make a harmony "not rarefied/ Nor fined for the in-
hibited instruments/ Of over-civil stops" (CP, 35).

Crispin's desire to compose reality is, for Stevens,
every man's need and one that must be satisfied individually. Each man's music is a unique ordering of the
"polyphony" of his experience. The hero disapproves
of those who cannot make distinctions between indi-

viduals, and who are content with "the lute/ As the marimba . . ." (CP, 38). But the lute is *not* the marimba, and man can find himself only in "the effortless and inescapable process of his own individuality" (NA, 46). Like Whitman, each man must make and sing a song of himself because, to counter Donne, each man is an island, living in "island solitude":

> The responsive man,
> Planting his pristine cores in Florida,
> Should prick thereof, not on the psaltery,
> But on the banjo's categorical gut.   (CP, 38)

At the end of "The Comedian as the Letter C," after Crispin has crossed the sea of self in order to discover the innate harmonies of the world, the hero accepts reality as the "insoluble lump" which he can never hope to change or shape to his own will. The world is now a crude turnip and "the fatalist/ Stepped in and dropped the chuckling down his craw,/ Without grace or grumble" (CP, 45). The hero's loss is, paradoxically, his gain because once he is resigned to his inability to dominate the world, or even the self, the hero can hear, if not the music of the spheres, the musical forms that abound in nature. His world becomes:

> perfectly revolved
> In those portentous accents, syllables,
> And sounds of music coming to accord
> Upon his lap, like their inherent sphere,
> Seraphic proclamations of the pure
> Delivered with deluging onwardness.   (CP, 45)

This deluge of music (combining as it does both images of sea and music) is a consummation, even though the poet considers the possibility that the music may "stick," that it may, like the romantic's inspiration, fail to arrive every day. Nevertheless, the poet reveals in this musical accord—even if it be temporary—the goal to which poetry should aspire. Crispin has become conscious of his own limitations, the ultimate failure of art to dominate nature, and this knowledge brings with it his individual style, for as Henri Focillon writes: "Human consciousness is in perpetual pursuit of a language and a style. To assume consciousness is at once to assume form." [7] Crispin does assume consciousness, and though he ends up a "profitless philosopher," he finds in the music of poetry the means of knowing himself and of effecting a liaison with his environment. Reality is finally triumphant because the world's music is heard and echoed, not composed. Consciousness is assumed, not willed. It is this knowledge that is "worth crossing seas to find," the knowledge that Stevens shares with Blake: "God is in me or else is not at all (does not exist)" (OP, 172).

Just as Stevens looks on the statue image as dead form when lacking the imagination and as living art when quickened by the shaping power of the imagination, so he finds that music must be felt or imagined before it truly exists. In "Peter Quince at the Clavier" (CP, 89– 92), the poet investigates the disparity between true musical form and the collection of noises that is often mistaken for art. The conflict is represented by Susanna, whose innocent imagination enables her to hear the music that marries her to her world, and the elders, whose sensuality and imaginative poverty limit them to physical sounds. Peter Quince is aware of an accepted principle of art: [8]

> Just as my fingers on these keys
> Make music, so the selfsame sounds
> On my spirit make a music, too.
>
> Music is feeling, then, not sound . . .

In the second part of the poem, Susanna achieves a
proper balance or fusion of imagination and reality, but
she does not become, consequently, some abstract,
ideal creature, divorced from the body. She *feels* the
"green water, clear and warm," but the music she discovers is not restricted by the senses because her
consciousness has probed until it found "Concealed
imaginings./ She sighed,/ For so much melody." Melody
and the imagination become one, and the power that
results from that union enables her to be at home in her
environment, until even "the winds were like her
maids . . . ." Like Eve before the fall, she is the world
she moves in, until the arrival of the serpent of fact:
"She turned—/ A cymbal crashed,/ And roaring horns."
After her "fall," her Eden becomes a world of noise; the
harmony is shattered:

> Soon, with a noise like tambourines,
> Came her attendant Byzantines.
> . . . .
> Anon, their lamps' uplifted flame
> Revealed Susanna and her shame.
>
> And then, the simpering Byzantines
> Fled, with a noise like tambourines.

Like the serpent in paradise, the Byzantines desert her,
leaving her to bear her "shame" alone. Stevens does not,

I feel, blame the elders for Susanna's downfall—they
are Blake's Songs of Experience that must accompany
Song of Innocence—but their limitation to the fact of
the body prevents them from realizing its imaginative
power.

The final section of the poem is Stevens' attempt to
make the fall fortunate. If the imagination is music, and
if the materials out of which it grows, on which it must
operate, are the sensual noises of actual experience,
how can the two be separated? The poet finds that the
beauty of imaginary music exists only when it is incarnated. Stevens' approach to platonic dualism is
neither to escape the flesh nor to deny the mind: he sub-
stitutes Nietzsche's "eternal recurrence" of the physical
world as a surrogate for the immortality of the soul. The
elders are touched by Susanna's music, but because they
are limited to a world of fact their "bawdy strings" cannot respond to sounds of the spirit. They cannot hear
even the continual harmonies of the natural world; they
hear "only Death's ironic scraping." The celebration of
change is Stevens' music, an art which partakes of the
reality it both shapes and expresses. The abstraction
"beauty" finds life only in the particulars of experience:
in bodies, gardens, evenings, and "a wave, interminably
flowing." The innocent song of Susanna remains pure,
but it is the "maiden's choral" that is immortal, not the
maiden. As in Keats's "Ode," it is the nightingale's
voice and not the nightingale that is perpetual: "The
voice I hear this passing night was heard/ In ancient days
by emperor and clown."

"The Man With the Blue Guitar" (CP, 165–84) is
Stevens' most extensive exploration of the ordering
power of poetry-as-music and the necessary balance

that art maintains, though momentarily, between the imagination and reality. The guitar gives form to feelings [9] that otherwise remain as chaotic as the monster "reality"; it creates a shape for the flux of emotions, symbolized by the sea, and it "brings the storm to bear." Stevens' paradox is a central one: One must tame reality and yet not deprive it of its wild power. The poet fears what Eliot calls "undisciplined squads of emotion," but he equally fears (and in this he resembles Whitman) the cage of artificial form which enervates emotions by isolating them from "the chaos and barbarism of reality." Perhaps the analogue here, as for the Statue image, is Keats's "Ode on a Grecian Urn." The "unheard music" may be superior to that received by the "sensual ear," but the urn's pure form can also be cold and unappealing. The blue guitar is "a form" — without which life is chaos — but its "strings are cold." Stevens uses an object as a meeting ground for form and content, but he finds stasis only in moments of musical epiphany when things exist "beyond the compass of change,/ Perceived in a final atmosphere."

Section XIX of "The Man With the Blue Guitar" is a microcosm of the whole poem, expressing the central theme on which Stevens works variations: [10] the need for seeing imagination and reality as separate forces, as monsters continually opposing each other, as forces that enjoy a truce only in the music of the guitar (i.e., poetry):

> That I may reduce the monster to
> Myself, and then may be myself
>
> In face of the monster, be more than part
> Of it, more than the monstrous player of

> One of its monstrous lutes, not be
> Alone, but reduce the monster and be,
>
> Two things, the two together as one,
> And play of the monster and of myself,
>
> Or better not of myself at all,
> But of that *as its intelligence,*
>
> Being the lion in the lute
> Before the lion locked in stone.   (CP, 175) [My italics.]

Stevens clarified the meaning of the poem when he wrote: "I want to face nature the way two lions face one another . . . I want, as a man of the imagination, to write poetry with all the power of a monster equal in strength to that of the monster about whom I write." [11] Moreover, Stevens would demand of the poet an orphic power, capable of giving voice and intelligence to insensate nature. Just as he later provides articulation for the rock of physical fact, he attempts to release the power that is confined in the "inanimate, cold forms" that Coleridge saw as "nature" without man's life-giving imagination. He would create a magic flute whose sounds would reduce the monster to at least temporary compliance and, paradoxically, free it to realize itself more fully. The lion is in the lute, the imagination is in man. But the power of nature cannot free itself without the poet's help. As Shelley wrote in *Prometheus Unbound:*

> Language is a perpetual orphic song,
> Which rules with Daedal harmony a throng
> Of thought and forms, which else senseless
>   and shapeless were.   (IV, i, 415)

In "The Man With the Blue Guitar" Stevens' tribute to the "shaping spirit" of music is somewhat undermined by the poet's awareness of the temporary and fragile nature of his moments of arrested harmony.[12] As with the image of the moon, which frequently suggests weakness, artifice, or impotence as well as the life-giving strength of imagination, the guitar's "corrupting" pallors and coldness can falsify or distort reality as well as order it. The detachment of the artist from the physical world is never the satisfying answer;[13] Stevens still yearns for "the relentless contact" (CP, 34) and not the vicarious, secondary enjoyments of art:

> I stand in the moon, and call it good,
> The immaculate, the merciful good,
>
> Detached from us, from things as they are?
> Not to be part of the sun? To stand
>
> Remote and call it merciful?
> The strings are cold on the blue guitar.   (CP, 168)

The chords of the guitar, like metaphor in general, can be a rationalization of reality, a thing of the mind, self-created, self-delusive. Crispin desired to merge with the sea, to lose himself in the physical scene or in society ("Society is a sea" [OP, 169]) and to leave his introspective self behind, to become one with his surroundings as "men in waves become the sea." Art, the player of the guitar finds, can be a source of alienation:

> It is the chord that falsifies.
> The sea returns upon the men, . . .
> . . . .
> The discord merely magnifies.   (CP, 171)

The resolution of the poet's dilemma that the poem
finally reaches is this: the music of the guitar, i.e., poetry,
is "issue and return," an intercourse between inner and
outer worlds, between the often ugly reality "oxidia" [14]
and an impossible utopia or "olympia." The two exist
together, one an actual fact, the other an insatiable need,
so that the repeated phrase "things as they are" comes
to mean an alternating current between actuality and a
fictional realm, a current which never ceases. Crispin
initially sees himself as "fluctuating between sun and
moon," between the real and the imagined. But, for
Stevens, the two are only separable in the mind; in
poetry they can be happily—but usually only fortui-
tously—combined. [15] The music of life becomes a duet
between God and the undertaker:

> A few final solutions, like a duet
> With the undertaker: a voice in the clouds,
>
> Another on earth, the one a voice
> Of ether, the other smelling of drink, . . .
> . . . .
>   the voice
> In the clouds serene and final, next
>
> The grunted breath serene and final,
> The imagined and the real, thought
>
> And the truth, Dichtung and Wahrheit, all
> Confusion solved, as in a refrain
>
> One keeps on playing year by year,
> Concerning the nature of things as they are.
>   (CP, 177)

The rarefied voice of the imagination ("God and the imagination are one" [CP, 524]) joins the grunted breath of the undertaker, smelling of drink and mortality. There can be no true musical harmony with one voice alone, even if the voice is God's. Reality is not only the tranquilizing palms of Key West but also the noxious smokestacks of New Jersey. "Things as they are" includes both and all, "the complicate, the amassing harmony."

The creative act itself, represented by the human voice, becomes the force that vies with the reality of the sea in "The Idea of Order at Key West" (CP, 128–30). Poetry, as distinguished from a poem, is the subject of a meditation which ends with an eloquent assertion of the power of the human imagination not to impose an intellectual order on reality but to invoke the music inherent in it.

Like other poems that juxtapose the sea and the human, this one is not transcendental, neither is it "symbolist." The poet claims early in the poem that "the sea was not a mask." To Baudelaire, a higher reality lurked mysteriously behind the objects of our perception, and art was simply the means of effecting a union with that higher reality; therefore, he seems far closer to Eliot than to Stevens. If we can agree with C. M. Bowra that "seen in retrospect the Symbolist Movement in the nineteenth century in France was fundamentally mystical," [16] Stevens is only superficially a symbolist.

A "higher" reality, which Stevens speculates on but never finally accepts, is at the heart of most symbolist poems, and perhaps the poems of Yeats and Eliot as well. But although the singer in "The Idea of Order at Key West" is clearly distinguishable from the reality she confronts, she is not an alien on the planet, largely

because she "makes" the world she desires — more ac-
curately, she *discovers* rather than *invents* what she
sees: [17]

> It was her voice that made
> The sky acutest at its vanishing.

She intensifies what is already there, so that the old
world seen and felt becomes, through the means of
song, a new world.

Yeats has written a somewhat similar poem, "A Crazed
Girl," in which a girl's music is her means for dealing
with the "bales and the baskets" that characterize the
squalor of her physical reality:

> That crazed girl improvising her music,
> Her poetry, dancing upon the shore,
> Her soul in division from itself
> Climbing, falling she knew not where,
> Hiding among the cargo of a steamship,
> Her knee-cap broken, that girl I declare
> A beautiful lofty thing, or a thing
> Heroically lost, heroically found.

> No matter what disaster occurred
> She stood in desperate music wound,
> Wound, wound, and she made it her triumph
> Where the bales and the baskets lay
> No common intelligible sound
> But sang "O sea-starved, hungry sea."

Both singers find in music the power to transform reality — or at least to make it tolerable. But the girl in Yeats's
poem is far from being integrated with her surroundings.
"Her soul in division from itself" yearns for a unity unat-

tainable in the "real" world; hence her "desperate music" can only serve as a diversion from the crude and the ordinary. That the girl does not *know* where she is climbing or falling, that the song she sings is "no common intelligible sound," suggests that Yeats is not completely satisfied with the music he praises. Moreover, that reality, the sea, yearns for some consummation beyond itself, attests to the poet's idealism and his doubts that poetry can achieve the harmonious integration of man and world. The poem further hints at the isolation of the artist whose limited "triumph" over reality leaves him still hungry.

In "The Idea of Order at Key West," however, the creative act is far from being a "desperate music" whose unintelligibility only increases the poet's sense of being severed from his platonic other-half. The singer's harmony with her surroundings brings the speaker of the poem to an awareness and knowledge of the interpenetration of imagination and reality. The boats, the night, the lights are unchanged by the singer's song; they remain what they are. But the speaker, like Gloucester in *King Lear*, has learned to see "feelingly," and the intensity of life is brought home to him:

> The lights in the fishing boats at anchor there,
> As the night descended, tilting in the air,
> Mastered the night and portioned out the sea,
> Fixing emblazoned zones and fiery poles,
> Arranging, deepening, enchanting night.

The words of the poem, in Stevens' phrase, "help us to live our lives," not by explaining life, whose demarcations must remain ghostly, but by responding to its own music, its "keener sounds."

Another analogue to Stevens' poem is, as some critics have noted, Wordsworth's "The Solitary Reaper." In Wordsworth's poem the cuckoo's song comes "breaking the silence of the seas/ Among the farthest Hebrides" and, by analogy, the image of man expressed by the poet's song fills the vessel of nature. The silence of "lifeless forms" may be that ineffable condition to which the mystic aspires, but for Wordsworth and Stevens the silent sea is often what Auden calls "primordial, undifferentiated flux, the substance which became created nature only by having form imposed on it," [18] or the chaotic unconscious from which man awakes to a realization of the form-giving power of his own voice. In "Sunday Morning" the silence of death—and for Stevens the dead myth of Christianity, "the holy hush of ancient sacrifice"—is associated with the sea, and at the close of the poem it is again the human voice rising in song that breaks the silence. Although the wide water remains "inescapable," the poet finds in his human "chant" a shape for chaos and a consolation for his "island solitude."

The meditating woman of "Sunday Morning" confronts the sea of dead silence in the opening stanza. At first she thinks negatively, a victim of the alienating effects of "the Fall." She still yearns for some metaphysical permanence:

> The pungent oranges and bright, green wings
> Seem things in some procession of the dead,
> Winding across wide water, without sound.
> The day is like wide water, without sound,
> Stilled for the passing of her dreaming feet
> Over the seas, to silent Palestine,
> Dominion of the blood and sepulcher.

A loss of consciousness and a rejection of the rich, phenomenal world seem to Stevens essential requirements
of the Christian religion, and, unlike Eliot, he will not
attempt to reach across that "wide water" to join the
ineffable. The woman entertains the possibility of the
"imperishable bliss" of divine union, but it is the poet
who controls her meditation and provides the song of
celebration of the physical sun which returns man to
himself as a part of a perishable and mutable, yet a lively
world, one meriting not silent prayer but boisterous
devotion:

> Supple and turbulent, a ring of men
> Shall chant in orgy on a summer morn
> Their boisterous devotion to the sun, . . .
> Their chant shall be a chant of paradise,
> Out of their blood, returning to the sky;
> And in their chant shall enter, voice by voice,
> The windy lake wherein their lord delights,
> The trees, like serafin, and echoing hills,
> That choir among themselves long afterward.
> They shall know well the heavenly fellowship
> Of men that perish and of summer morn.
> And whence they came and whither they shall go
> The dew upon their feet shall manifest.

There is no meaning of a doctrinal kind in this passage,
although the pseudo-religious diction—paradise, chant,
choir, serafin, heavenly fellowship—leads one to expect
some. Man's song does not transcend him but creates a
"mythology of self"; it effects an acceptance of a world
which, like dew, is transitory yet recurring. The men's
chant to a male sun (of extraversion) ends the woman's
meditative wanderings (introversion); her retreat into
ideas about life is ended by an "orgy" of delight, an

incantation in which inner and outer worlds, sun and moon, male and female, are one. The final stanza restores the woman to the knowable world of things, of deer, quail, berries, and pigeons. As long as things are seen and felt and accepted, says Stevens, the inescapable wide water is bearable, and man's island solitude is enriched by the accompaniment of natural music. It is finally the "song" of things and not ideas about things that answers the questions of the woman in "Sunday Morning."

One of the problems that Wordsworth dealt with in *The Prelude* occurs in miniature in Stevens' "Tea at the Palaz of Hoon" (CP, 65): what is the proper relationship of man to the external world, of the maker of music to the sea? The figure of Hoon, who appears in two Stevens poems, is apparently one more persona for the solitary romantic artist, using the physical world as a means of knowing himself. At first Hoon thinks that the music he hears is outside, and he is quizzical not only about its position but also its significance:

> What were the hymns that buzzed beside my ears?
> What was the sea whose tide swept through me there?

But his doubts are resolved by the revelation that he creates the world he moves in, that he gives a shape to the sea of reality:

> Out of my mind the golden ointment rained,
> And my ears made the blowing hymns they heard.
> I was myself the compass of that sea:
>
> I was the world in which I walked, and what I saw
> Or heard or felt came not but from myself;
> And there I found myself more truly and more strange.

These lines from "The Idea of Order at Key West" are almost equivalent in meaning:

> For she was the maker of the song she sang.
> The ever-hooded, tragic-gestured sea
> Was merely a place by which she walked to sing.

Stevens sees in music the creative power of mind over nature or, more precisely, of mind *with* nature. Sharing Coleridge's theory of the "coalescence of an object with a subject," he equates himself with his world through an act of perception, and, as I. A. Richards wrote of Coleridge, "the perceiving and the forming are the same. The subject (the self) has gone into what it perceives, and what it perceives is, in this sense, itself. So the object becomes the subject and the subject the object." [19] Stevens further echoes Coleridge's belief that poetry is not common speech but perfected harmony, that the poet's power "reveals itself in the balance of reconcilement of opposite and discordant qualities [in Stevens these are embodied in a pattern of opposing images: e.g., north and south, sun and moon] . . . and while it blends and harmonizes the natural and the artificial, still subordinates art to nature."

In a late poem, "The Sick Man" (OP, 90), Stevens expresses the desire for this "reconcilement" of the two worlds of north and south, but the union is never realized except in the imagination, in the musical chords which will dissolve the distinction between interior and exterior reality. The south is elemental, spontaneous, revealing itself in music:

> Bands of black men seem to be drifting in the air,
> In the South, bands of thousands of black men,
> Playing mouth-organs in the night or, now, guitars.

The next stanza contrasts the northern world, and the
poet uses the word "remote" to suggest the isolation
that also characterizes the northern men in the earlier
"Arrival at the Waldorf" (CP, 240–41). The men act in
unison, their singing has movement and sound—but
no words. The south seems to have found its expression
in music whereas the north is passionate but inarticulate, as if the world of the mind has no language to express itself.

> Here in the North, late, late, there are voices of men,
> Voices in chorus, singing without words, remote and
>   deep,
> Drifting choirs, long movements and turnings of sounds.

The union of thought and passion can be achieved, it
seems, only by the imagination in isolation:

> And in a bed in one room, alone, a listener
> Waits for the unison of the music of the drifting bands
> And the dissolving chorals, waits for it and imagines
>
> The words of winter in which these two will come
>   together . . .

The remainder of the poem is a tribute to the artist who
turns within himself to discover the words which, for
the time of their existence, will harmonize winter and
summer, mind and physical world. Only through an
imaginative act can the unity of the imagination and
reality take place (as momentarily on the blue guitar),
and it is Stevens' belief that this "song" is sufficient to
"take the place of empty heaven and its hymns."

The two kinds of music considered in "Peter Quince
at the Clavier," imaginative music as opposed to literal

sounds, occur in other Stevens poems, and we find that the poet is not committed to either kind when divorced from the other. *Real* music becomes neither imaginary nor actual but a composite, and it is the music that the "gloomy grammarians" and the "funest philosophers and ponderers" in "On the Manner of Addressing Clouds" (CP, 55–56) can never find because they ignore the external world of changing seasons in the interest of cultivating an artificial language of the mind. By separating expression from the world of emotions it expresses ("reality is not that external scene but the life that is lived in it" [NA, 25]), they create an abstract formal music that is merely "exaltation without sound." They desert humanity and become creatures of cloud, with the "speech of clouds," and their denial of the physical world—they find nature's rhythms "stale"— makes their music flat and their world a "drifting waste" of poverty. Stevens advises the scholars to leave their books and find true knowledge in the seasons:

> These
> Are the music of meet resignation; these
> The responsive, still sustaining pomps for you
> To magnify, if in that drifting waste
> You are to be accompanied by more
> Than mute bare splendors of sun and moon.

A return to the material world and its music replenishes the "pomps" (splendor) of language, and restores gloomy and funereal thinkers to the wondrous "pomps" of nature which introspection has made poor. Again, it is in poetry that Stevens finds the means of restoring man to the glories of the world, a world without myth. Like the gloomy grammarians, the player of the blue guitar

knows that he is poor, but fortunately he realizes his
hope of recovery:

> The earth, for us, is flat and bare.
> There are no shadows. Poetry
>
> Exceeding music must take the place
> Of empty heaven and its hymns . . .   (CP, 167)

The same relationship between poetry and music is
found in "Mozart, 1935" (CP, 131–32), and the poet's
fictive music is heard against the voice of a world fast
approaching the catastrophe of total war. Stevens, far
from being an escapist, insists on a music that expresses
the present. In time of war the poet must assume "the
voice of angry fear,/ The voice of this besieging pain."
The present, with all of its "envious cachinnation," must
be the basis of art which without it is weak and ineffectual, a pleasant diversion:

> That lucid souvenir of the past,
> The divertimento;
> That airy dream of the future,
> The unclouded concerto . . .

Neither the anodyne of the past nor a soporific dream of
the future is acceptable to the poet, who must in the
present create the storehouse we turn to for sustenance,
in order to bear the world's essential poverty and the
pressures of external events. Stevens advises the poet, in
the person of Mozart, to continue his fictive music:

> If they throw stones upon the roof
> While you practice arpeggios,
> It is because they carry down the stairs
> A body in rags.

Just as the elders in "Peter Quince at the Clavier" could
hear "only Death's ironic scraping," so the poet's audience in its devotion to fact ignores — is even antagonistic
toward — the consolations art provides. In the midst of
war, the poet should be able to rise above transitory
events, and Stevens implores him to "be thou the voice,/
Not you." In other words, the poet should become the
voice of the "reality" of his own time, but still express
more than the merely local.[20] Mozart continues to make
his imagination ours because music is not bound by
events or time. His music, like earth's music, survives
all of man's attempts to make this a universe of death:

> We may return to Mozart.
> He was young, and we, we are old.
> The snow is falling
> And the streets are full of cries.
> Be seated, thou.

T. S. Eliot, faced with the same formless present, in
which music is replaced by discordant "cries," turned
to the past, and the Church, for an image of order. As the
poet said in "East Coker," "There is only the fight to
recover what has been lost." Stevens, as his use of the
statue image particularly reveals, rejects the view that
the past houses a shape for the present. The past for him
is a dead thing, and the artistic modes as well as the
world-views that once harmonized man and nature are
no longer viable. In "Sad Strains of a Gay Waltz" (CP,
121–22), for example, the poet uses the nineteenth-
century musical form as an image of an outgrown mode
of expression. Just as the minuet imaged the eighteenth-
century "rage for order," the waltz represented the
freedom from formal rigidity that the nineteenth-cen-
tury artist saw in neoclassicism. For Stevens, both are

lifeless because they no longer mirror a living age. We
listen to minuets, never dance to them, and perhaps the
waltz is approaching the time when it will be "so much
motionless sound":

> There comes a time when the waltz
> Is no longer a mode of desire, a mode
> Of revealing desire and is empty of shadows.
>
> Too many waltzes have ended. . . .

The intellectual schemes symbolized by minuet and
waltz have ended, and as Stevens looks around at the
"mobs of men" he finds that they desperately long for
harmony and order but that they create "without knowing how,/ Imposing forms they cannot describe,/ Requir-
ing order beyond their speech." The poet cannot accept
the validity of Eliot's "idea of order," because the past—
and it includes the Church—is now "empty of shadows,"
it is out of the present sun's demands and rewards. (Stevens consistently uses "shadow" in a favorable sense,
suggesting the half-light of uncertainty and change
which he feels is the limit of man's knowledge.) The
poem "Sad Strains of a Gay Waltz" ends with a plea for
a new musician,[21] a musician of our time who can discover a music that will be our "mode of desire," which
will join us to each other, not in a traditional faith but
in a shared doubt. It will deny all past myth and yet
affirm existence:

> The epic of disbelief
> Blares oftener and soon, will soon be constant.
> Some harmonious skeptic soon in a skeptical music
>
> Will unite these figures of men and their shapes
> Will glisten again with motion, the music
> Will be motion and full of shadows.

As with Yeats's image of the dancer, men will fuse with their expressive form, and Stevens himself will be the "harmonious skeptic" who will, in the role of the poet, "supply the satisfactions of belief, in his measure and in his style" (OP, 206). Stevens maintains a secular vision. As he said in one of his adagia: "The relation of art to life is of the first importance especially in a skeptical age since, in the absence of a belief in God, the mind turns to its own creations and examines them, not alone from the aesthetic point of view, but for what they reveal, for what they validate and invalidate, for the support that they give" (OP, 159).[22]

Because, as Peter Quince declared, "music is feeling then, not sound," we find Stevens the maker of language again bound by a paradox: How can he find an image, a name, for that powerful irrational effect which music has over us and yet not limit that effect by translating it? As Susanne Langer says, "it seems peculiarly hard for our literal minds to grasp the idea that anything can be *known* that cannot be *named*."[23] Unlike poets who approach the ineffable by discarding the ballast of concrete imagery, Stevens attempts to satisfy the human need for naming in "To the One of Fictive Music" (CP, 87–88). The poet realizes that man "apprehends the most which sees and names,/ As in your name, an image that is sure," but the poem articulates a problem rather than a solution. Stevens in this poem is far from successful: The "one" of fictive music remains "one," despite the poet's semantic search, which leads him from direct statement through simile and metaphor, in an attempt to provide his muse a local habitation and a name.

The opening stanza is more incantation than definition.[24] By employing "and" eleven times in eight lines, Stevens hopes to accumulate meanings around a central female image which is the indescribable spirit of music.

She is both sister and mother, lover and queen, "and
flame and summer and sweet fire," but because she is
imaginary, these analogies fail to do more than suggest
her protean nature. She is built up out of human terms
(just as Stevens later will evoke "the fictive man created
out of men" [CP, 335]), and although perfect form, she
is "out of our imperfections wrought."

There is, Stevens realizes, a music of the literal, actual
world, but it carries alone none of the fulfilling power of
fictive music. By being true-to-life, it is consequently
crude, divisive, alienating:

> Now, of the music summoned by the birth
> That separates us from the wind and sea,
> Yet leaves us in them, until earth becomes,
> By being so much of the things we are,
> Gross effigy and simulacrum . . .

This is inferior music because, like the music of the red-
eyed elders, it is limited to the physical realm which can
only be a "gross effigy," merely a material vessel empty
of the life that the imagination provides. Nature and art
conflict only when the imagination is absent for, like
Coleridge, Stevens believes that fictive music, a creation
of the imagination, must reconcile the opposites of art
and nature. As he says in his preface to the *Collected
Poems* of William Carlos Williams, "Something of the
unreal is necessary to fecundate the real" (OP, 256), so
by a willing suspension of disbelief we accept the "one
of fictive music," and thereby "give ourselves our likest
issuance."

After what Eliot calls a "raid on the inarticulate," the
poet deserts the search for an image adequate to express
imaginary music. All similes, too, fail to "correspond"

to the idea Stevens has in mind, and so he reverses his
field: instead of demanding the "near, the clear" from
his muse, he accepts the impenetrable obscurity of his
source and is content with the "strange unlike" which
defeats all simile. Death, like fictive music, is cloaked in
darkness yet is able to provide intensity, if not meaning,
to man's life. "Death is the mother of beauty," and the
unknown fecundates the known. Fictive music is also
"of the fragrant mothers the most dear." The poet, therefore, asks the archetype (celestial or interior paramour)
to descend into the human realm, bringing imaginative
riches that are heightened by being set against mortality:

> On your pale head wear
> A band entwining, set with fatal stones.
> Unreal, give back to us what once you gave:
> The imagination that we spurned and crave.

Stevens demands that his spiritual music exist in the
physical world, and he will not finally allow himself to
be satisfied with music as the perfect image for poetry.
Because poetry, by employing words and not notes, is
anchored in a world of denotation, the poet must face
the "reality" of an impure language that only at times
reaches the condition of music. Mallarmé believed that
poetry must sever its connections with crude reality
before it could ever discover itself. "Certain arts, such as
music," he wrote, "use difficult signs which make them
mysterious for the layman. Music has its secrets; *why
then should not poetry?*"[25] But for Stevens, defective
as they are, words come closer to representing the
flawed creature who employs them than do musical
notes; hence the noted lines, "Poetry/ Exceeding music
must take the place/ Of empty heaven and its hymns,/

Ourselves in poetry must take their place" (CP, 167), must be reread, emphasizing the word "exceeding." Stevens would probably agree with Susanne Langer that "because the forms of human feeling are much more congruent with musical forms than with the forms of language, music can *reveal* the nature of feelings with a detail and truth that language cannot approach." [26] Nevertheless, he would face the futility of purging language of its nonmusical or discursive aspects. Even when glorifying music, Stevens frequently selects images of vocal music (hymn, choir, chant, choral) rather than the purely symbolic "signs" that Mallarmé hoped to discover by divorcing poetry from prose. Just as Stevens will later reject the metaphoric disguises for the barrenness of actual fact in *The Rock,* so he realizes that the imperfect world is final and accepts "the essential prose/ As being" (CP, 36). Neither a Platonist nor a Transcendentalist, the poet says:

> The imperfect is our paradise.
> Note that, in this bitterness, delight,
> Since the imperfect is so hot in us,
> Lies in flawed words and stubborn sounds.   (CP, 194)

Language, as Heraclitus found, was "the most constant thing in a world of ceaseless change, an expression of that common wisdom which is in all men; and for him the structure of human speech reflects the structure of the world." [27] For Stevens, also, the sound of words sometimes seems to be a reality in itself, a defense against the pressures of disorder from within as well as without. Thus the poem "Description without Place" (CP, 339–46) explores the "reality" of language:

Thus the theory of description matters most.
It is the theory of the word for those

For whom the word is the making of the world,
The buzzing world and lisping firmament.

It is a world of words to the end of it,
In which nothing solid is its solid self. (CP, 345)

The poet's experience is not, however, unique; he simply brings to the level of consciousness the knowledge that we and our world are inescapably flawed. His special skill is his ability to fashion a "world of words" that gives acceptable form but not a meaning to the "exhalations of the sea" (CP, 144) and the "meaningless plungings of water and the wind" (CP, 129). The poet becomes the artist described by R. G. Collingwood in his *Principles of Art:* "a person who comes to know himself, to know his own emotion. This is also knowing his world, that is, the sights and sounds and so forth which together make up his total imaginative experience. The two knowledges are to him one knowledge, because these sights and sounds are to him steeped in the emotion with which he contemplates them: they are the language in which that emotion utters itself to his consciousness. His world is his language. What it says to him it says about himself; his imaginative vision of it is his self-knowledge." [28] But it is Stevens' hope that the poet's quest for an articulated consciousness may have more than individual value:

As part of nature he is part of us.
His rarities are ours: may they be fit
And reconcile us to our selves in those

> True reconcilings, dark, pacific words,
> And the adroiter harmonies of their fall.   (CP, 144)

The relationship between music and the sea reveals again Stevens' difficulty in making categorical choices. If the poet were consistent in opposing human speech and inarticulate reality, his imagery would fall into a manageable pattern, but the poet's words are not always seen as superior to the sounds of external nature, crude as they may be: both seem to originate in a single "vital music" (CP, 259), that existed before artificial compositions. What the poet longs for is a language uncorrupted by logic or syntax:

> Speak, even, as if I did not hear you speaking,
> But spoke for you perfectly in my thoughts,
> Conceiving words,
>
> As the night conceives the sea-sounds in silence,
> And out of their droning sibilants makes
> A serenade.   (CP, 86)

Being willing to live with "sound without meaning" (CP, 421) and "a flow of meanings with no speech" (CP, 431), the poet admits that words are, at times, truly secondary to natural sounds:

> How pale and how possessed a night it is,
> How full of exhalations of the sea . . .
> All this is older than its oldest hymn . . .   (CP, 144)

The poet as maker alternates with poet as appreciator; unable to merge with original and elemental power, the musician becomes a listener and no longer seeks that

bliss submerged beneath appearance,
In an interior ocean's rocking
Of long, capricious fugues and chorals.   (CP, 79)

Bliss remains submerged and one is left with the capricious compositions of nature.

In Stevens there are two oceans: "the ocean of the virtuosi" and "the ugly alien" (CP, 156). The sea in "Sea Surface Full of Clouds" (CP, 98–103) is an ugly alien that must grow calm or still before the impersonal virtuoso can project his imaginative conflicts on a reflecting surface. Stevens is content in this poem to record the benign drama that reaches no final act. The poet is more interested in revealing the "transfigurings" of the sky and sea, imagination and reality, than he is in restlessly probing after a first cause. In the French refrain, the poet does attempt to name the power that both entertains and consoles mankind, as he evoked the "One of Fictive Music" who is "summoned by the birth/ That separates us from the wind and sea,/ Yet leaves us in them . . ." (CP, 87). But accepting the paradox that a surface can be full, Stevens stops short before a naked reality, accepting the limitations of metaphor.

> The nakedness would rise and suddenly turn
> Salt masks of beard and mouths of bellowing,
> Would – But more suddenly the heaven rolled
>
> Its bluest sea-clouds in the thinking green,
> And the nakedness became the broadest blooms,
> Mile-mallows that a mallow sun cajoled.   (CP, 101)

On the verge of becoming antagonistic, reality is tamed by a fortuitous change of weather.

Stevens can be, as Keats described the poet, "the most

unpoetical of all God's Creatures," and the passive
speaker of "Sea Surface Full of Clouds" apparently
allows the natural forces of sea and sky to play without
interference. The imagination, in the first stanza, does
evolve and *diffuse* the resemblances that give pleasure;
however in all of the remaining stanzas the imagination's
role is simply to observe—to feel or hear—natural phenomena. The things of the world possess the power of
acting and interacting, one "conjuration trumped" by
the arrival of another. Stevens' impersonality here is
contrived so that the reader can confront his own reality
more directly. He wrote in one of his essays:

We say that the sea, when it expands in a calm and immense
reflection of the sky, resembles the sky, and this statement
gives us pleasure. We enjoy the resemblance for the same
reason that, if it were possible to look into the sea as into glass
and if we should do so and suddenly should behold there some
extraordinary transfiguration of ourselves, the experience
would strike us as one of those amiable revelations that nature
occasionally vouchsafes to favorites.   (NA, 80)

The poem ends with "fresh transfigurings of freshest
blue."

Yet the poet is not truly outside the poem, and behind
the facade of objective presentation the workings of the
imagination are defined. It is capable of bringing unity
out of diversity (sea and clouds can become sea-clouds)
but more importantly it has the power of dispelling the
"sinister" and "malevolent" aspects of nature, freeing
colorful surfaces from "shrouding shadows":

and then blue heaven spread

Its crystalline pendentives on the sea
And the macabre of the water-glooms
In an enormous undulation fled.   (CP, 100)

Reality, as represented by the sea, can be slopping, sinister, malevolent, dark. The imagination's "blue heaven," with its "sovereign clouds," can transform "sea-glooms" into "sea-blooms" and can even be capable of "resisting or evading the pressure of . . . reality . . ." (NA, 26). Darkness can be balanced by color, morbidity by health, death by creativity:

> So deeply sunken were they that the shrouds,
> The shrouding shadows, made the petals black
> Until the rolling heaven made them blue,
>
> A blue beyond the rainy hyacinth,
> And smiting the crevasses of the leaves
> Deluged the ocean with a sapphire blue.   (CP, 100–01)

In "Anecdote of the Jar" (CP, 76) the opposition of human creativity and natural life is overtly presented, but here, without the intrusion of the artifact, the interpenetration of imagination and reality is revealed. Neither is finally triumphant, the fiction is never chosen over the fact:

> Then the sea
> And heaven rolled as one and from the two
> Came fresh transfigurings of freshest blue.   (CP, 102)

The two roll *as* one but *are* two, just as the "sea of spuming thought" (CP, 13) is different from the actual ocean.

In "The Idea of Order at Key West" the singer and the "dark voice of the sea" retain their individual identities, and only in the consciousness of the third parties is any interpenetration possible. The external world of "grinding water and gasping wind" creates sounds, words without the pattern we call language. For the moment of the song, the sea assumes an order or "self" not its own, one that will end, whereas:

> There will never be an end
> To this droning of the surf.   (CP, 23)

The singer's knowledge is, sadly, bought at the expense of ignoring the world as fact, and it is significant that the lights of the fishing boats, not the music, "mastered the night and portioned out the sea . . .". Only after the song has ended is the speaker able to realize that his belief incorporates words, words of the sea, and a third entity which is the unruly sea itself. The sea can be mastered, finally, by consciousness, but a self-created "world" of song is a fiction that Stevens never accepts for long.

Stevens longs for an essence with which to merge, but the unity of classical or Christian myth is not viable. The Paltry Nude—as opposed to the ideal "goldener nude"—must confront a present sea, without the support of archaic myth. Discontented with her "meagre" surface play, she seeks the "interiors of the sea" (CP, 5–6). The poet's reason constantly hopes to fix the "wavering water" of external nature but there is "A beating and a beating in the centre of/ The sea" (CP, 354) that will not be stilled. Triton, in "The Comedian as the Letter C," embodies the element he represents and therefore his personal gestures are the gestures of reality.

> Could Crispin stem verboseness in the sea,
> The old age of a watery realist,
> Triton, dissolved in shifting diaphanes
> Of blue and green? A wordy, watery age
> That whispered to the sun's compassion . . .   (CP, 28)

To name Scylla and Charybdis, for the ancients, was to order and contain the natural hazards and to keep voyagers from being, as Crispin was, "washed away by magnitude." Stevens, knowing that past myths are inactive, confronts real forces which the names once served:

> Triton incomplicate with that
> Which made him Triton, nothing left of him,
> Except in faint, memorial gesturings,
> That were like arms and shoulders in the waves,
> Here, something in the rise and fall of wind
> That seemed hallucinating horn, and here,
> A sunken voice, both of remembering
> And of forgetfulness, in alternate strain.   (CP, 28–29)

The poet no longer believes in Triton, but he can still humanize the force outside himself by creating resemblances: the waves are like arms and shoulders; their rise and fall are like remembering and forgetting. One of the significant stages in Crispin's worldly education occurs when the poet manqué rejects the "distortion of romance" and realizes that the sea "severs not only lands but also selves. Here was no help before reality" (CP, 30). Although in the end he accepts a cabin instead of "loquacious columns by the ructive sea" he has been "made vivid by the sea." Despite his final fadedness, he has lived an extensive and intensive life, confronting reality, not being content with "the snug hibernal from that sea and salt." He returns to land, a family, to "social nature," but one feels that, like Ishmael or Prospero, his return to the community of man may be no final solution to his conflicts, that the voyager should be ready for further sea excursions.

Myths continue to yield before the superior force of "reality" throughout Stevens' poetry so that in a late poem like "The River of Rivers in Connecticut" (CP, 533) Charon is unavailable to ferry the poet across to any ultimate meaning. Like Crispin, Stevens has only found a "mythology of self" and the river of rivers (ironically opposite to the platonic "idea" of river) is not metaphysical but is actually located in Connecticut. It satisfies what Stevens calls in "St. Armorer's Church from the Outside" (CP, 529–30), "the need to be actual and as it is":

> In that river, far this side of Stygia,
> The mere flowing of the water is a gayety,
> Flashing and flashing in the sun. On its banks,
>
> No shadow walks. The river is fateful,
> Like the last one. But there is no ferryman.
> He could not bend against its propelling force.

The power of the physical world, like the sun's creative energy, must remain beyond man's control—his attempts to know by "naming"—yet within his range of appreciation. Stevens is like the man Marianne Moore describes:

> Man looking into the sea,
> taking the view from those who have as much right
>   to it as you have to it yourself,
> it is human nature to stand in the middle of a thing,
> but you cannot stand in the middle of this. . . .

To say that Stevens is a poet of surfaces may indicate his acceptance of human limitations, his humility before the ineffable God he calls "reality." He accepts the *vif* of the river, which is "not to be seen beneath the appearances/ That tell of it," and the towns whose "meaning" is also concealed beneath colorful surfaces that glisten and shine and sway. Like the sea, the river is unfathomable; but in this it resembles Stevens' world which he calls "my green my fluent mundo" (CP, 407) or his life "that is fluent" (CP, 222). The river is a particular of that world, a mirror of Narcissus.

> It is the third commonness with light and air,
> A curriculum, a vigor, a local abstraction . . .
> Call it, once more, a river, an unnamed flowing,
>
> Space-filled, reflecting the seasons, the folk-lore
> Of each of the senses; call it, again and again,
> The river that flows nowhere, like a sea.

Stevens' "abstraction" is clearly no disembodied idea; it is grounded in the local, but it remains unnamed because to name it is to make it exclusively local, forgetting that the real can be "made more acute by an unreal" (CP, 451). Ultimate truth remains secure beneath the surface, but we "sense" it, acknowledging that the river, like the sea of the unconscious, gives us mysterious intimations of ourselves while keeping its own identity intact.

4 THE STATUE AND THE WILDERNESS

"One walks easily

The unpainted shore, accepts the world
As anything but sculpture."

So-and-So Reclining on Her Couch

Wallace Stevens made few concessions to clarity, not because he enjoyed obscurity but because he was unable to accept any purely rational or intellectual system which the poems could simply express. In poem after poem, he dramatized his imaginative concerns by employing images as characters, and the conflict resulting from the juxtaposition of disparate images was far more interesting to him (and closer to his conception of "real" life) than any denouement, any resolution of tensions leading to an overt statement of theme or belief. His poetic method was similar to the critical method of R. P. Blackmur, who once said that he liked to put one thing beside another, to see what happened.

The statue, one of Stevens' recurring images, frequently appears in conjunction with the wilderness of external nature, the disorder of experience. Bronze, marble, stone, effigy are but a few of the variables of this image which I have arbitrarily limited; and Africa, the American South (Florida, Carolina), and the jungle are associated with Stevens' wilderness. The interplay between these opposing forces reveals much about Stevens' conception of poetic form, the relationship of the human imagination to the reality upon which it operates. Just as Stevens preferred experiencing life to defining it, he preferred images that shifted their meanings; the reader may suddenly find that a sign for one complex of emotion is indicating a contradictory one. The poet's changing attitude toward his own images creates a problem for the critic who makes his analysis on the basis of only a few appearances of an image or who works within a single context.[1] In an early lecture the poet forewarns the reader to avoid taking his images in only one way. Before he begins reading he says: "The poem is called 'The Old Woman and the Statue.' The old woman is a symbol of those who suffered during the depression and the statue is a symbol of art, although in several poems of which *Owl's Clover,* the book from which I shall read, consists, the statue is a variable symbol" (OP, 219).

Stevens often uses the statue image to suggest fixity in a world of incessant change, but unlike Keats's urn, which imitates reality and is consequently separate from it, or Yeats's Byzantium, which presents an image of transcendent reality, the statue is almost exclusively seen as dead form, "cold" or metallic, "marble" or "bronze," unappealing when seen against the backdrop of the vivid natural world. Thus, as a symbol of art the image is misleading; more often, it is art manqué, art without the vitalizing power of the imagination.

Such a statue is "the great statue of the General Du

Puy" (CP, 391–92) in *Notes toward a Supreme Fiction*.
Because Stevens sees life as a process not a product, the
statue seems ludicrous, following as it does the poet's
praise of the "green" world of lovers and bees. The
description suggests that any finality in art associates
it with the past (which, Stevens feels, must be dead to
the living) or with a devitalized present:

> The right, uplifted foreleg of the horse
> Suggested that, at the final funeral,
> The music halted and the horse stood still.
>
> On Sundays, lawyers in their promenades
> Approached this strongly-heightened effigy
> To study the past, and doctors, having bathed
>
> Themselves with care, sought out the nerveless frame
> Of a suspension, a permanence, so rigid
> That it made the General a bit absurd,
>
> Changed his true flesh to an inhuman bronze.
> There never had been, never could be, such
> A man.

Again Stevens is unlike Keats or Yeats in that he will
entertain no idea of permanence that requires the ar-
resting of process, and he will accept no definition of
form that is not based on feeling.

> There is a feeling as definition.
> How could there be an image, an outline,
> A design, a marble soiled by pigeons?   (CP, 278)

Yeats could momentarily be content with a vision of "a
marble or a bronze repose" and Keats with the Greek

myths. But for Stevens even the highly imaginative
pagan myths are rejected when they become solidified
in an ideal realm outside the mutable world. In "An
Ordinary Evening in New Haven," for example, after
the "statue of Jove" has been blown up and the sky has
quieted, the world can be enjoyed for what it is, a free
world that the weight of the statue subdued:

> There was a clearing, a readiness for first bells,
> An opening for outpouring, the hand was raised:
> There was a willingness not yet composed,
>
> A knowing that something certain had been proposed,
> Which, without the statue, would be new,
> An escape from repetition, a happening . . .   (CP, 483)

After the destruction of Jove, the air is cleared of permanence, and the poet can declare, *"C'est toujours la
vie qui me regarde. . . ."*
 In the same poem Stevens uses the statue (the man of
bronze) to help reveal one of his major themes: man's
need to accept change as permanent, to find comfort in
the realization that he is a part of a harmonious natural
cycle:

> We say of the moon, it is haunted by the man
>
> Of bronze whose mind was made up and who, therefore,
>   died.
> We are not men of bronze and we are not dead.
> His spirit is imprisoned in constant change.
>
> But ours is not imprisoned. It resides
> In a permanence composed of impermanence,
> In a faithfulness as against the lunar light,

> So that morning and evening are like promises kept,
> So that the approaching sun and its arrival,
> Its evening feast and the following festival,
>
> This faithfulness of reality, this mode,
> This tendance and venerable holding-in
> Make gay the hallucinations in surfaces.   (CP, 472)

This theme is pervasive in Stevens and its most revealing analogue is, perhaps, Keats's "To Autumn."

Keats's poem comes after the other great odes in
which the poet meditated the relation between the
ideal and the real, permanence and change. And, like
Stevens, he celebrates the world in concrete terms
while accepting his own mortality, his own "identity"
with his surroundings. He constructs a poem from the
materials of external nature, personifying transience
itself, and the fear of change which caused him to be
attracted to a "cold pastoral" on the static urn (comparable to Stevens' statue image) was overcome. Keats
matures into an acceptance of the season of decay and
dissolution, and he builds this "idea" into his descriptive detail.[2] Although the poet does not intrude into his
picture, the final images are charged with his personal
awareness of time and his identification with natural
process:

> Then in a wailful choir the small gnats mourn
> Among the river sallows, bourne aloft
> Or sinking as the light wind lives or dies;
> And full-grown lambs loud bleat from hilly bourne;
> Hedge-crickets sing; and now with treble soft
> The red-breast whistles from a garden-croft;
> And gathering swallows twitter in the skies.

Here is no Truth-Beauty equation; neither are we teased out of thought. The love of the created world leads to resignation, not renunciation. Ripeness is all.

Keats's ending is like many endings of Stevens' poems, particularly like that of "Sunday Morning":

> Deer walk upon our mountains, and the quail
> Whistle about us their spontaneous cries;
> Sweet berries ripen in the wilderness;
> And, in the isolation of the sky,
> At evening, casual flocks of pigeons make
> Ambiguous undulations as they sink,
> Downward to darkness, on extended wings.   (CP, 70)

A red-breast whistles in Keats; the quail whistle in Stevens. Gnats sink in Keats; pigeons sink in Stevens. But the sense detail serves a similar purpose: it comes after meditation and speculation on ideas of immortality, to reestablish the poet's position in the changing world of nature. "The faithfulness of reality" is Stevens' abiding faith. The artificial form of the statue is closer to death than to life, for the idea of the human condition is lessened by artificial form, "The marbles are pinchings of an idea . . ." (CP, 276). Like Henri Focillon, Stevens believes that "form is not only, as it were, incarnated, but that it is invariably incarnation itself." [3] To understand man truly, one must seek his image in his world and not in his art, his statuary:

> He is what he hears and sees and if,
> Without pathos, he feels what he hears
> And sees, being nothing otherwise,
> Having nothing otherwise, he has not
> To go to the Louvre to behold himself.   (CP, 194)

Stevens generally regards the statue as a definition, an image of the made-up mind; hence, his use of the image reveals his rejection of dogmatic thinking and affirms his kinship with some of the writers gathered under the broad wing of "Existentialism." Camus, for example, at the conclusion of his discussion of absurd reasoning in *The Myth of Sisyphus*, says simply: "The preceding merely defines a way of thinking. But the point is to live." And, earlier, Dostoyevsky in *Notes from the Underground* objects to the rationalists' need for certainty:

And who knows (it is impossible to be absolutely sure about it), perhaps the whole aim of mankind in striving to achieve on earth merely lies in this incessant process of achievement, or (to put it differently) in life itself, and not really in the attainment of any goal, which, needless to say, can be nothing else but twice-two-makes-four, that is to say, a formula; but twice-two-makes-four is not life, gentlemen. It is the beginning of death.

Stevens' similar comments on definition in the poems, as well as in the essay "The Noble Rider and the Sound of Words," help to clarify the poet's attitude toward the statue image. Moreover, his aversion to definition explains why Stevens' poems are, in general, variations on themes, rather than strictly developed forms. He writes in the essay:

I am evading a definition. If it is defined, it will be fixed and it must not be fixed. As in the case of an external thing, nobility resolves itself into an enormous number of vibrations, movements, changes. To fix it is to put an end to it. Let me show it to you unfixed.   (NA, 34)

Because Stevens believes that "the imagination is the life of things" and that it is in the changing mind of man that a work of art is realized, he finds it difficult to look favorably on most works in stone, marble, or bronze. This difficulty, however, only indicates an aversion to a limited conception of form, not to form itself. He shares Focillon's sense of dynamic form:

Whether constructed of masonry, carved in marble, cast in bronze, fixed beneath varnish, engraved on copper or on wood, a work of art is motionless only in appearance. It seems to be set fast – arrested, as are the moments of time gone by. But in reality it is born of change, and it leads on to other changes.[4]

The statues compared in "The Noble Rider and the Sound of Words" make it possible for Stevens to praise the work of Verrocchio because it is imaginative, hence alive, while condemning a Clark Mills statue of Andrew Jackson because it is only stone:

The statue is neither of the imagination nor of reality. That it is a work of fancy precludes it from being a work of the imagination. A glance at it shows it to be unreal. The bearing of this is that there can be works, and this includes poems, in which neither the imagination nor reality is present. (NA, 11)

In general, Stevens' attitude toward statuary is negative; the image becomes a sign for a limited conception of form. As I hope to show, his distrust of definition becomes a distrust of any traditional view of form. Art is finally subordinate to nature.

Like Valéry, Stevens considers the act of writing poetry more important than the completed poem; in fact, for both artists, a completed poem would contradict their theory by establishing a rational order, a fixity. "A work is never necessarily *finished*," writes Valéry, "for he who made it is never complete." [5] And elsewhere the French poet declares, "A work is never *complete . . .* but *abandoned*." [6] The loose structure of "Le Cimetière Marin" is paralleled by the uncertain, tentative stanzas of many of Stevens' poems, for example "Sunday Morning," a similar meditation which partakes of the shifting "reality" it deals with. Stevens' negative use of the statue leads to an enlarged understanding of form itself, effecting a true statue which is neither stone nor marble, brass nor bronze, but a changing thing existing simultaneously in the external world and in the mind of man. If the poet sometimes yearns for the positive assurance that fixed form offers, he is merely speculating, in the hope of seeing real man more clearly: "Just to know how it would feel, released from destruction,/ To be a bronze man breathing under archaic lapis . . ." (CP, 425).

We encounter the authentic statue in "The Old Woman and the Statue" (OP, 43–46), a part of *Owl's Clover,* Stevens' longest poem, which he omitted from his *Collected Poems,* but which I shall explore in considerable detail because it is related to other poems. We also see what happens when the human mind and imagination refuse to preceive the heightened sense of reality that the statue provides. In this poem the central figure is able to transform the living art into "marble hulk" by her own limited vision. Just as a bad work of art is a distortion of reality, so a limited imagination can deaden a good work of art. The artist who created the statue was imaginative and therefore had anticipated that his creation would exist in a world of change. A part of the light, the clouds, the autumn leaves that "raced

with the horses in bright hurricanes," the work of art is
not merely marble; it is more than a product of the craft
theory of art. The sculptor who made it revealed more
than technique:

> More than his muddy hand was in the manes,
> More than his mind in the wings.

The imagination gives life to the statue, even though
the leaves, the "rotten leaves," attest to a cycle outside
it, one that will survive men and statues. The juxtaposition of statue and leaves, art and reality, engenders life,
as each partakes of the other.

It is the "black" mood of the woman, however, that
reduces the external scene to fixity. She is "unmoved"
by the physical world, and, like Coleridge in "Dejection: An Ode," she sees but does not feel because
"Wings/ And light lay deeper for her than her sight."
Unlike the singer in "The Idea of Order at Key West,"
she has a negative response to external things. Whereas
the singer by the sea is able to bring form out of "the
meaningless plungings of water and the wind," she can
only misshape an order inherently there. After her
arrival on the scene:

> The mass of stone collapsed to marble hulk,
> Stood stiffly, as if the black of what she thought
> Conflicting with the moving colors there
> Changed them, at last, to its triumphant hue . . .

Here is Stevens' tribute to the power of the human mind:
It can shape external reality to its own will. The woman
anchors herself in a world of fact; she becomes the fixity
that the true statue contradicts. She persists in her mood:

> A mood that had become so fixed it was
> A manner of the mind, a mind in a night
> That was whatever the mind might make of it . . .

Finally, after the woman departs, the statue and its background reality return to life. Unhampered by her ponderous imagination, the horses "rise again," and the poem ends:

> The light wings lifted through the crystal space
> Of night. How clearly that would be defined!

The definition is clear, but paradoxically, it is a definition of feeling, not of idea.

Stevens returns to his usual negative or distrustful use of the statue in the next poem from *Owl's Clover,* "Mr. Burnshaw and the Statue" (OP, 46–52). The poem opens with "The thing is dead . . ." and continues with a condemnation of any art that expresses an idea divorced from a living context. Such a creation is a product of the rational, theoretical mind, lacking the vitality the imagination can provide when in harmony with the changing present; it is ludicrous, "gawky plaster" or a "thing from Schwarz's," merely a work of fancy which is

> Ugly as an idea, not beautiful
> As sequels without thought.

The poem was conceived, we are told, as a retort to the social-conscious critics of the thirties, Stanley Burnshaw in particular, who lamented Stevens' refusal to deal with pressing political or social problems in his poetry.[7] Stevens' haughtiness and snobbery seem no more objectionable than that of Eliot or Yeats, but his involvement with the imagination-reality struggle rather than the class struggle, his refusal to commit himself to political causes, combined with his persistently playful idiom, made his position particularly vulnerable. Communism was to him a "grubby faith" and he was unwilling to play a "'Concerto for Airplane and Pianoforte,'/ The newest Soviet reclame" (OP, 62). He was to write much later, although his conviction arrived far earlier: "I might be expected to speak of the social, that is to say sociological or political, obligation of the poet. He has none" (NA, 27). Stevens' hauteur is like that of Mallarmé, who feared the disastrous effects of democracy on poetry:

Let the masses read works on moral conduct; but please don't let them ruin our poetry. Oh, poets, you have always been proud; now be more than proud, be scornful! [8]

Stevens opposes any system of thought, whether it be Christianity or communism, which imposes a single meaning on experience. "There is no such thing as the truth" (CP, 203), he believes, only momentary perceptions of a controlling order, a number of possible truths. The statue image is useful to the poet in suggesting the monotony or sterility of dogmatic belief, of "the railway-stops/ In Russia at which the same statue of Stalin greets/ The same railway passenger . . ." (CP, 367). An ironic vindication of Stevens' position is that "the" particular truth embodied in the statue of Stalin is a truth no longer, but a part of the dead past. What remains in the world are men weak in imagination, who submit to dogmas. Exuberant life outlasts the cries

> Of those for whom a square room is a fire,
> Of those whom the statues torture and keep down.
>   (CP, 191)

Stevens' method in "Mr. Burnshaw and the Statue" is typical: he juxtaposes the statue, representing cold sterile order, with the quickening changes of the physical world. Images of transience are played off against the dead stone; plowmen, peacocks, doves, leaves, wind, damsels move around the statue in a "chaos that never ends." The poet is hospitable to chaos — one persona is a "Connoisseur of Chaos" — and he believes that man can triumph over the disorder of experience, not by creating a dead artifact, an imitation of life that can only be a poor copy, never "real," but by accepting life's inherent order, discovering epiphanies or momentary arrestings of process, more valuable because more rare. The speaker of "Mr. Burnshaw and the Statue" realizes that "So great a change is constant" and that "the temple [the work of art] is never quite composed." But in its movement art resembles life itself:

> But change composes, too, and chaos comes
> To momentary calm, spectacular flocks
> Of crimson and hoods of Venezuelan green
> And the sound of z in the grass all day, though these
> Are chaos and of archaic change.

Stevens is traditional — despite his frequent rejection of tradition — in seeing the poetic act in terms of song, and in the concluding sections of "Mr. Burnshaw and the Statue" he combines song with dance to reveal the power of human beings to oppose fixity. The poet directs humanity to:

> Dance, now, and with sharp voices cry, but cry
> Like damsels daubed and let your feet be bare
> To touch the grass and, as you circle, turn
> Your backs upon the vivid statue.

After celebrating the physical delights of being human, the poet proclaims the incredible power of the human imagination, the transforming effect of an "act of the mind":

> Conceive that while you dance the statue falls . . .

Thus fixity is overcome and Stevens has answered his critics in terms of the poetic act itself, which he represents, as Valéry does, by the dance. "It goes nowhere," wrote Valéry, who developed an analogy that would offend any Marxist critic, or any critic demanding the *utile* in art:

> If it pursues an object, it is only an ideal object, a state, an enchantment, the phantom of a flower, an extreme of life, a smile — which forms at last on the face of the one who summoned it from empty space.
>
> It is therefore not a question of carrying out a limited operation whose end is situated somewhere in our surroundings, but rather of creating, maintaining, and exalting a certain *state*, by a periodic movement that can be executed on the spot; a movement which is almost entirely dissociated from sight, but which is stimulated and regulated by auditive rhythms.[9]

Stevens' dance resembles Valéry's in that it "goes nowhere," but it does make something happen. During the time of its life, the dead certainties are overcome for, as Stevens says elsewhere, "Life is the elimination of what is dead" (OP, 169).

Stevens never entertained the possibility of transcending his bodily form and achieving some Byzantium of the mind. As Frank Kermode has pointed out, the static qualities associated with Byzantine art are possible "only when the vision and not the world is the object of man's consideration." [10] With Stevens, the world is always the base from which he aspires and to which he returns. In "Memorandum" (OP, 89) he says:

> Say this to Pravda, tell the damned rag
> That the peaches are slowly ripening.
> Say that the American moon comes up
> Cleansed clean of lousy Byzantium.

In Byzantium Yeats suggests a possible resolution of the conflict between permanence and change: an artist can become his work of art, a statue. The tension between art and nature relaxes only when process is eliminated. Kermode's description of Yeats's visionary realm is useful in showing us what Stevens' realm is not:

In this paradise life, all those delighting manifestations of growth and change in which the scarecrow has forfeited his part, [sic] give way to a new condition in which marble and bronze are the true life and inhabit a changeless world, beyond time and intellect (become, indeed, the image truly conceived, without human considerations or cost). The artist himself may be imagined, therefore, a changeless thing of beauty, purged of shapelessness and commonness induced by labour, himself a self-begotten and self-delighting marble or bronze. [11]

Yeats yearned for a "marble or a bronze repose," but Stevens agrees with Heraclitus that "It is in changing that things find repose."

The contrast between "statue" and "dance" in "Mr. Burnshaw and the Statue" is productive of meaning because both are art forms, although one is transitory, the other permanent. Stevens' preference for the living form over the dead one is unmistakable, especially if we keep in mind other poems in which the same contrast exists. "Life Is Motion" (CP, 83), for example, a poem from *Harmonium,* could well serve as a text, since the title itself indicates the Heraclitean dance by which the poet characterizes life, as well as art.

> In Oklahoma,
> Bonnie and Josie,
> Dressed in calico,
> Danced around a stump.
> They cried,
> "Ohoyaho,
> Ohoo" . . .
> Celebrating the marriage
> Of flesh and air.

Here, the image of the statue is foreshadowed by the stump, the dead fixity that the human imagination contradicts. Yeats's "Great rooted blossomer," an image of natural wisdom and unity of being, was also juxtaposed with the art form of the dance in which Yeats found intimations of ideal form. The poverty of Stevens' world in his poem (the "calico," the "stump") only serves to intensify the exuberance, the brio, of the dancers. The nonsense they utter is fully satisfying because reasonable language could never express the unreasonable joy that man can experience when he is joined not to God, not to his fellowman, not to a restricting belief, but to the atmosphere of which he is a part. The dancers enter the Dionysiac state Nietzsche describes, in which one merges with the thoughtless universe.[12]

Perhaps the best example from the early poems of the yoking of "statue" and "dance" is in "Dance of the Macabre Mice" (CP, 123). This ironic poem, super-

ficially lighthearted, contains an opposition central to
an understanding of Stevens' thought:

> In the land of turkeys in turkey weather
> At the base of the statue, we go round and round.
> What a beautiful history, beautiful surprise!
> Monsieur is on horseback. The horse is covered
>   with mice.
>
> This dance has no name. It is a hungry dance.
> We dance it out to the tip of Monsieur's sword,
> Reading the lordly language of the inscription,
> Which is like zithers and tambourines combined:
>
> The Founder of the State. Whoever founded
> A state that was free, in the dead of winter,
>   from mice?
> What a beautiful tableau tinted and towering,
> The arm of bronze outstretched against all evil!

Stevens chooses the commonplace, trivial image of mice
to represent a transience that is, paradoxically, permanent, whereas man's enduring monuments to his own
self-importance survive but become outdated, ludicrous (as, for example, the monument to Stalin in "Mountains Covered with Cats" [CP, 367–68]). The "hungry
dance" of the mice is meaningful natural form, which is
also an art form, fulfilling itself in a vivid present. *Actual*
mice will outlast, the poet says, all monuments to any
ideal, and no artificial form, even of bronze, can have
an effect on the "evil" (or as he says elsewhere the
"mal") in life. Truth can never be, in reality, embodied.
As he says in another poem:

> The idols have seen lots of poverty,
> Snakes and gold and lice,
> But not the truth . . . (CP, 204)

The statue can be form without content, whereas the hunger of the mice is the meaning of their motion, and the quixotic gesture of the statue against the imperfections in life becomes only a tableau, a "tinted" artifice against which mice enjoy existence. The mice are a part of a regenerative reality; the statue is a solidification of reality. Hence the mice are only ironically macabre since they, in effect, comprehend things as they are. Their spontaneity is a kind of health, and as Stevens says in "Parochial Theme" (CP, 191–92):

> This health is holy,
> This halloo, halloo, halloo heard over the cries
>
> Of those for whom a square room is a fire,
> Of those whom the statues torture and keep down.

The ending of "Mr. Burnshaw and the Statue" is a triumph of change, of human utterance over the "words that are the speech of marble men." Heraclitus again affords us a parallel. He found in the image of fire his most satisfying analogue for the human condition, for life itself. It assumes forms, but the forms are not lasting; life was for him, as for Shakespeare, "consum'd with that which it is nourish'd by." Stevens employs this image of transience to end his poem, while establishing his commitment to this mutable planet. He advises his celestial paramours (which resemble his "interior paramour" and his "one of fictive music") to reject the arti-

ficial form of the statue and to return to the physical
world:

> That is yourselves, when, at last, you are yourselves,
> Speaking and strutting broadly, fair and bloomed,
> No longer of air but of the breathing earth,
> Impassioned seducers and seduced, the pale
> Pitched into swelling bodies, upward, drift
> In a storm blown into glittering shapes, and flames
> Wind-beaten into freshest, brightest fire.   (OP, 52)

It is the motion, the glitter, the brightness, and the freshness of life that are valuable; any attempt to elucidate
life's meaning may turn us all, like Medusa's victims,
into stone.

The next poem in *Owl's Clover*, "The Greenest Continent" (OP, 52–60), takes the reader out of the civilized
world where statues are thought to incorporate man, and
into the "wilderness" where statues are less familiar,
more incongruous. It is characteristic of Stevens to bring
the two poles of art and nature into a relationship that
helps to enrich each. The decadent world of Europe is
left behind,[13] and in Africa, where the "idea" of permanence is unknown, where death replaces heaven as
finality, the poet discovers an effective image to contrast
with the statue: the serpent, which in its yearly changes
of skin symbolizes the cyclical pattern of the natural
world. The poet speculates on the effect of art on the
luxuriant jungle:

> If the statue rose,
> If once the statue were to rise, if it stood,
> Thinly, among the elephantine palms,
> Sleekly the serpent would draw himself across.
> The horses are a part of a northern sky
> Too starkly pallid for the jaguar's light . . .

Here the poet faces "reality" directly, without reliance upon either art or God ("No god rules over Africa"), and he is able to exist in the presence of extraordinary richness, without thought of past or future, both of which he associates with the statue's realm of "common-places" and "common dreams." Be free of the restrictions the statue represents, Stevens seems to tell us, and seek no ultimate or lasting meanings. Certainties are truly dead certainties because

> The statue belongs to the cavernous past, belongs
> To April here and May to come. Why think,
> Why feel the sun or, feeling, why feel more
> Than purple paste of fruit, to taste, or leaves
> Of purple flowers, to see? The black will still
> Be free to sing, if only a sorrowful song.

One of the human failures that Stevens associates with sculpture is man's adherence to outworn attitudes or modes of thought. Images out of the past do not satisfy our immediate needs, yet when we look at ourselves expressed in much of contemporary art, we are also disappointed. The fault, Stevens would say, is not with the world we live in but with our imaginations which, in accepting the old or adhering to the commonplace, fail in shaping the raw material of our experience. In "Lions in Sweden" (CP, 124–25), for example, Stevens refuses to accept the traditional virtues represented by the stone lions or *Fides, Justitia, Patientia,* and *Fortitudo;* neither will all the timeworn phrases, which label these embodied abstractions, speak for the poet. But after Stevens' rejection of past forms, the soul "still hankers after sovereign images," and in order to satisfy its hunger, the poet must, as Pound said, make it new. His art must be personal, local, evolved from his environments:

> If the fault is with the lions, send them back
> To Monsieur Dufy's Hamburg whence they came.
> The vegetation still abounds with forms.

Stevens ends this poem, as he does the majority of his poems, by returning man to external nature while isolating him from his past history; in this approach he seems akin to Coleridge and Wordsworth, who in rejecting the established forms ("statuary") of the Augustans hoped to revitalize poetry, to use the imagination to integrate man and physical nature (Wordsworth) and to reconcile the opposites of art and nature (Coleridge). For Stevens, the eighteenth-century world of Claude ("a world that was resting on pillars./ That was seen through arches") is no longer our world because

> The pillars are prostrate, the arches are haggard,
> The hotel is boarded and bare.   (CP, 135)

What worked once can never work again. When looking toward the past, Stevens, unlike the Augustans, sees a "cemetery of nobilities," a museum of perfectly lifeless statues. As he says in "The Noble Rider and the Sound of Words":

in our present, in the presence of our reality, the past looks false and is, therefore, dead and is, therefore, ugly; and we turn away from it as from something repulsive . . .   (NA, 35).

Stevens refuses to "play the flat historic scale"; and when looking over the graves of his ancestors in "Dutch Graves in Bucks County" (CP, 290–93) he directly denies a classical belief:

> And you, my semblables, in gaffer-green,
> Know that the past is not part of the present.

Stevens' rejection of history as a means of knowing man
and reconciling him to his condition is further intensi-
fied by his rejection of *communitas*. He refuses to write
an Essay on Man; rather, like Wordsworth, he will only
record the growth or development of his individual
mind, divorced from the past and his contemporaries:

> What was the purpose of his pilgrimage . . .
> If not, when all is said, to drive away
> The shadow of his fellows from the skies,
> And, from their stale intelligence released,
> To make a new intelligence prevail?   (CP, 37)

In "Recitation After Dinner" (OP, 86–88) Stevens speculates on the idea of tradition and attempts to define the
term, to give it "form." But because the poet's conception of form is fluid, he employs his images of "marble"
and "bronze" to indicate what tradition is not. Striving
for definition, Stevens is, at the same time, avoiding the
commitment that definition demands. The poet longs to
embrace tradition:

> But the character
> Of tradition does not easily take form.
>
> It is not a set of laws. Therefore, its form
> Is not lean marble, trenchant-eyed. . . .
> . . . .
> The bronze of the wide man seated in repose
> Is not its form. Tradition is wise but not
> The figure of the wise man fixed in sense.

Stevens' distaste for fixity again allies him with Henri
Focillon, for both writers agree that form is an aspect of
the mind which changes constantly because the mind

changes. "Our minds are so filled with the *recollection of forms*," writes Focillon, "that we tend to confuse them with the recollection itself, and therefore to believe that they inhabit some insubstantial region of the imagination or the memory, where they are as complete and as definite as upon a public square or in a museum gallery." [14]

The worthwhile statue is, then, alive only when it exists in change, and only when its creator creates in conjunction with a living reality and anticipates changes to come. An artist should not construct an artifact, like Yeats's golden bird,[15] removed from the shifting wind and light, but should fuse the artificial with the natural. As we saw in "The Old Woman and the Statue," Stevens reveals how art can properly express form:

> So much the sculptor had foreseen: autumn,
> The sky above the plaza widening
> Before the horses, clouds of bronze imposed
> On clouds of gold, and green engulfing bronze,
> The marble leaping in the storms of light.   (OP, 43)

The metamorphosis of clouds into gold and bronze is nature assuming form, and the "marble leaping" is artifice quickened by the living forms around it. Again, Focillon parallels Stevens when he says that "between nature and man form intervenes. The man in question, the artist, that is, forms his nature; before taking possession of it, he thinks it, feels it, and sees it as form." [16]

In section five of "A Duck for Dinner" (OP, 60–66), the fourth poem in *Owl's Clover*, Stevens again defines the true work of art, the statue that is more than stone. Because the sculptor reveals living images in a physical world, he expresses rather than creates form. In the tradition of humanism, "The statue is the sculptor not the stone" (OP, 64). External nature has been assimilated, so to speak, and for this reason a viewer will see *his* world and, through the sculptor's imagination, *himself* expressed.

> The sprawlers on the grass
> See more than marble in their eyes, see more
> Than the horses quivering to be gone, flashed through
> With senses chiseled on bright stone. They see
> The metropolitan of mind, they feel
> The central of the composition, in which
> They live. They see and feel themselves, seeing
> And feeling the world in which they live.

Stevens' emphasis on the emotions, the senses (the *seeing* and *feeling*, rather than the rational mind) as the means of comprehending the world is pervasive in his work, and here we see that for him a genuine work of art is a never-ending collaboration between man and nature, a mingling in which the artist serves as catalyst. Life, to Stevens, is in the end more important than art, and "the operation of the imagination in life is more significant than its operation in or in relation to works of art . . ." (NA, 146). The task of the artist faced with an unruly reality is not to invent forms but to discover "ideas of order" and to share them with others. He must not impose order on life; he must try to illuminate through his imagination a changing world that can never be held by one system of belief. Stevens shares Wordsworth's view, in the Preface to *The Lyrical Ballads*, that "there is no object standing between the poet and the image of things." Once he has experienced that image, the poet has a responsibility to his fellowman that is not social or political, but is moral nevertheless:

I think that his function is to make his imagination theirs and that he fulfills himself only as he sees his imagination become the light in the minds of others. (NA, 29)

Two well-known poems that enlarge our understanding of the imagination-reality conflict, and focus on the images of human artifice in contrast to images of natural order, are "Connoisseur of Chaos" and "Anecdote of the Jar." Both are concerned with the ordering power of the mind in relation to the disorderly reality it can never quite dominate.

In "Connoisseur of Chaos" (CP, 215–16) Stevens brings aesthetic and critical judgment to bear on experience, to support, in effect, one of his own aims: "To live in the world but outside of existing conceptions of it" (OP, 164). The poised, disinterested speaker considers two possible ways of dealing with reality: to impose rational order on experience, or to discover an imaginative order inherent in it. The first would require a logical system of thought, a definition of "the" truth, which would limit life's possibilities; the second would be closer to Keats's life "proved on the pulses" and hence would not be any reasonable order. Stevens' aversion to fixity appears again as statuary, and the dialectic of the poem aims at proving that all propositions about life are subordinate to life itself. Each proposition is held tentatively, making the play and the movement of the poem, but no conclusion is reached, a *relationship* is the poem's ultimate meaning.

The first proposition, "A violent order is disorder," represents the violence of any orthodoxy that refuses to tolerate change; it is a Bed of Procrustes which distorts reality to fit a plan, and it transforms life into statuary. As we have seen, Stevens entertains no nostalgia for the past or for any order that is not created out of today's chaos. Hence, he could well be alluding to Eliot's belief in the "letter" of the law, and his belief that "the present is directed by the past," when he says,

> We cannot go back to that.
> The squirming facts exceed the squamous mind.

In "Of Modern Poetry" (CP, 239–40), Stevens opens with a similar response to a past when men submitted to dogma:

> The poem of the mind is the act of finding
> What will suffice. It has not always had
> To find: the scene was set; it repeated what
> Was in the script.

To attempt to impose a past system of thought on the present is to do violence to reality, for Stevens believes that one should work with the "squirming facts" and attempt to build one's order from them. As he says in "The Comedian as the Letter C," "his soil is man's intelligence," meaning that any satisfying philosophy or aesthetic must evolve from a consideration of the natural world, must account for nonrational happenings which we both observe and participate in.

The second proposition, "A great disorder is an order," does not simply give man license to surrender to a meaningless chaos or to deny his innate need for formulated meaning. Instead, it provides a way of "seeing" in the disorder surrounding man "forms" which repeat and reassure, satisfying man's need for more than hedonistic delight. Having rejected the "meanings" of tradition and orthodoxy, of whatever sort, the speaker comes back to what is before him, the inescapable facts:

It is April as I write. The wind
Is blowing after days of constant rain.
All this, of course, will come to summer soon.
But suppose the disorder of truths should ever come
To an order, most Plantagenet, most fixed . . .

By accepting the non-sense of nature, the cycle of the seasons, one finds what permanence man can know. But man can only "suppose" (imagine) that nature's endless repetition can become as fixed as statuary. Actually, one dominates chaos by accepting it, for "the man-hero is not the exceptional monster,/ But he that of repetition is most master" (CP, 406). This proposition is not, however, the consummate answer either because the mind still longs for an absolute, still hungers for meaning beyond the facts.

Both propositions are finally only something to think about; neither is "the" truth. But by avoiding final answers, the poem says, we make ourselves accessible to the power of transient answers:

Now, A
And B are not like statuary, posed
For a vista in the Louvre. They are things chalked
On the sidewalk so that the pensive man may see.

Ideas about life must not be solidified into "philosophy" but must remain tentative, and the chalk image, like images of snow and autumn leaves in other poems, points to a meaning that does not survive the physical reality it momentarily clarifies. Although both rational approaches fail at presenting a comprehensive, unified meaning for experience, they do, in conjunction, generate "relation":

> And yet relation appears,
> A small relation expanding like the shade
> Of a cloud on sand, a shape on the side of a hill.

But the "relation" is ambiguous; it can only be sensed, not fully comprehended; it is like the "fluttering things" that have "so distinct a shade" which is the only order found by the speaker of "Le Monocle de Mon Oncle." The pensive man can *see* the two ideas because he has extrapolated them from chaos; he has insight:

> The pensive man . . . He sees that eagle float
> For which the intricate Alps are a single nest.

By identifying himself with a creature without cognition (Stevens at other times assumes the voice of wind, sea, mountain), the speaker, as pensive man, transcends his own limitations momentarily and sees the world purged of man's divisive speculation, his A's and B's. The eagle can transform the watchmaker's intricacy of the Alps into a unified, simple habitation because it cannot conceive of life as statuary. The poem does not end where it began, in the mind; the speaker has learned all that he can surely know about the world: that it is simply his home, the place where he lives.

We see the conflict or tension between images of human artifice (statuary) and the wilderness (the chaos of reality) most clearly in the "Anecdote of the Jar" (CP, 76), a poem that has probably elicited as much comment as any of Stevens' poems. As usual, the wilderness is "reality," what Stevens calls "things as they are." The jar, however, is not simply an artifact, a dead creation, statuary; it suggests imaginative creation, the ordering power of the imagination. Few critics have had difficulty spotting and finding names for the two forces that meet on the hill, but most feel compelled to resolve the conflict in favor of one or the other, not considering the pattern of imagery into which the poem fits.

As we saw in "Connoisseur of Chaos," a *relation* can be the meaning of a poem, and in "Anecdote of the Jar" Stevens also presents an opposition but never finally chooses a side. As in numerous poems, the imagination acts as a stabilizing order which contrasts with the process of external nature. Yet the jar which symbolizes this human power is gray and bare, suggesting more of what Stevens calls "poverty" than the enriching imagination, more of fancy than a "shaping spirit." Moreover, even though the wilderness is "slovenly" and reduced to sprawling, it still possesses a vitality the sterile jar lacks, for the jar

> did not give of bird or bush,
> Like nothing else in Tennessee.

The poet's ambivalence is remarkably similar to that of Keats in his "Ode on a Grecian Urn," in which the poet strives to escape the human condition ("A burning forehead") only to find that the imaginative realm ("Cold Pastoral!") is equally distasteful. Arguments continue as to whether Keats devises a resolution to his dilemma or whether he abdicates choice. If Douglas Bush is correct that "reality" would be a close gloss for "truth" in the Truth-Beauty equation,[17] then we find Keats and Stevens again in agreement that the natural world, "things as they are," is form. In contrast, Eliot's Chinese jar in "Burnt Norton" seems to be separated from the temporal world; its form is coldly ideal:

Words move, music moves
Only in time; but that which is only living
Can only die. Words, after speech, reach
Into silence. Only by the form, the pattern
Can words or music reach
The stillness, as a Chinese jar still
Moves perpetually in its stillness.

Because Eliot believes that there is "only a limited value/ In the knowledge derived from experience," [18] he is fundamentally mystical, attempting to reach beyond poetry. His jar, consequently, enjoys no context.

Stevens' poem contains no overt statement that could be interpreted as a preference for either the imagination or reality. The jar, as either work of art ("statue") or symbol for imaginative power, is unproductive in a natural sense; yet it does affect or change the natural world by its very existence. It is like the music of the blue guitar which the player realizes is finally ineffectual in subduing reality (in "The Man With the Blue Guitar" represented by "sea" or "storm" rather than "wilderness"):

I know my lazy, leaden twang
Is like the reason in a storm;

And yet it brings the storm to bear.
I twang it out and leave it there. (CP, 169)

It is, therefore, the power of the jar to bring the wilderness *to bear* that is the theme of the poem. The either/or choice between nature and art labored by critics is misleading and, moreover, alien to the poet who spent a lifetime celebrating the love affair but not the marriage of imagination and reality. As the poet wrote in "The Noble Rider and the Sound of Words":

the relation between the imagination and reality is a question, more or less, of precise equilibrium. Thus it is not a question of the difference between grotesque extremes.   (NA, 9)

And elsewhere in the same essay, after advising the poet that "he cannot rise up loftily in helmet and armor on a horse of imposing bronze," Stevens chooses *both* imagination and reality:

he will find that it is not a choice of one over the other and not a decision that divides them, but something subtler, a recognition that here, too, as between these poles, the universal interdependence exists, and hence his choice and his decision must be that they are equal and inseparable.   (NA, 24)

In "Conversation with Three Women of New England" (OP, 108–09), published a year before the poet's death, we find Stevens still concerned with the statue and the wilderness of reality, still refusing to commit himself to one or the other. In fact, believing with Blake that "the Eye altering alters all," he presents three personae who express differing ways of dealing with the problem. The first woman believes that there is a transcendent unity, a controlling force outside life, a "sole, single source and minimum patriarch." The second introduces the conflict between the natural and the man-made, focusing on statuary. She believes that things created by the human mind are as "natural" as anything in the external world:

So that a carved king found in a jungle, huge
And weathered, should be part of a human landscape,

That a figure reclining among columns toppled down,
Stiff in eternal lethargy, should be,
Not the beginning but the end of artifice,
A nature of marble in a marble world.

The second woman would seem to share Jacques Maritain's belief that the creative artist does not compete
with God in rival creation, but simply extends God's
creation.[19] Even without being aware of the differing
viewpoints of Maritain and Stevens, however, we can
detect in the imagery — prepared as we are by the poet's
previous uses of "marble" — a distasteful tone which
undercuts the woman's theory. The "things of the mind/
Should be as natural as natural objects," and the marble
figures "should be,/ Not the beginning but the end of
artifice . . ." but in actuality they are not. What the
woman reveals is a "weathered" carving, an edifice in
ruin, a figure "stiff in eternal lethargy." Man as artist
ever fails to fix the changing materials of reality. Finally,
the third woman expresses a view of romantic individ-
ualism which denies God, sees man's limitations as
self-imposed, and affirms man's need to see himself
without the consolations offered by religion or art:

The author of man's canons is man,
Not some outer patron and imaginer.

Stevens, in a customary manner, considers the three
viewpoints (man as God, man as artist, man as man), but
in his conclusion he makes no choice, effects no final
synthesis. The poem ends tentatively, with a question:

In which one of these three worlds are the four of us
The most at home? Or is it enough to have seen

And felt and known the differences we have seen
And felt and known in the colors in which we live,
In the excellences of the air we breathe,
The bouquet of being — enough to realize
That the sense of being changes as we talk,
That talk shifts the cycle of the scenes of kings?

As one would predict, Stevens entertains the possibility of sharing each world-view, and in a vital way he does, since each woman presents an aspect of his own thought. But he agrees least with the woman who would convert nature to marble, man to an image of man. That "carved king found in a jungle," like that "placed" jar in Tennessee, is only a means, not an end, only a device to help us "sense" the magnitude of the reality we confront, and provide us with the knowledge that the "colors" that surround us are more satisfying than the whitest marble.

We see, by Stevens' ambiguous handling of the statue image, especially in *Owl's Clover*, that it is unsatisfactory as a means of conveying the poet's conception of art, largely because he will not isolate artistic from natural creation. In order to distinguish a statue from the dead stone which in fact it is, Stevens gives it "feathery wings" or makes other transformations, metamorphoses,[20] which give it vitality. But the problem is never solved, nor could it ever be, because, unlike Yeats, the poet will not commit himself to an image divested of process. The statue must be changing before it can adequately image reality, but it can only change significantly in the imagination. Hence Stevens, in the final poem of *Owl's Clover* "Sombre Figuration" (OP, 66–71), admits the failure of the image by shifting his atten-

tion to a new one, the "subman," a vague figure suggesting the imaginative power existing in all of us, linking
us all together, a kind of god eternally engaged in perceiving the world anew. The poem opens:

> There is a man whom rhapsodies of change,
> Of which he is the cause, have never changed
> And never will . . .

He is that second self in us which, ignoring reason or
logic, achieves his life and continuity through our senses;
we prove his existence constantly "in what we see," "in
what we hear," in "a cry, the pallor of a dress, a touch."
That the image is a desperate attempt to find a happier
resolution to the poet's dilemma is fairly certain. Turning from stone to nebulous, archetypal spirit, the poet
discovers that he has no image at all. The "subman"
never appears again in a Stevens poem.

At the end of *Owl's Clover*, the statue still stands, but
it has become a troublesome reminder of the world's
body which remains firm and unknowable under its
changing appearances. All images or analogies fail to
indicate the right relation of art to the reality it shapes,
so the poet says farewell to the statue, farewell to the
subman, farewell to the evasions of the imagination:

> Even imagination has an end,
> When the statue is not a thing imagined, a stone
> That changed in sleep. It is, it is, let be
> The way it came, let be what it may become.

It is the unformed stone that Stevens chooses over art;
it is nature purged of man's images of it. The images,
like light, that played over the surface of life are sub-

dued ("Night and the imagination being one"), beyond
reason, the poet sees

> the rapture of a time
> Without imagination, without past
> And without future, a present time . . .

In this final use of the statue in *Owl's Clover*, Stevens
foreshadows *The Rock*, his final gathering of poems,
with its aura of serenity and acceptance of the world as
fact, with all fictional disguises laid aside; he anticipates
the time when he will no longer be dependent upon the
diversions of the imagination. His own words from "Effects of Analogy" clarify both poems:

Take the case of a man for whom reality is enough, as, at the
end of life, he returns to it like a man returning from Nowhere
to his village and to everything there that is tangible and visible, which he has come to cherish and wants to be near. He
sees without images. But is he not seeing a clarified reality of
his own?   (NA, 129)

Stevens admits by his dissatisfaction with the statue
image that what he has been striving for cannot be contained in any artificial form; in spite of the permanent
values that the statue represents, it demands at the same
time that the poet subordinate the very reality it is de-
signed to clarify. Stevens might agree with Walter Pater's Marius that

the radical flaw in the current mode of thinking would lie
herein: that, reflecting this false or uncorrected sensation,
it attributes to the phenomena of experience a durability
which does not really belong to them. Imaging forth from those
fluid impressions a world of firmly outlined objects, it leads

one to regard as a thing stark and dead what is in reality full of animation, of vigor, of the fire of life.[21]

Marius found that in confronting the external world directly (without the windows of religion or art, which create distortions) he had founded a religion of the "here and now" and lived his days "in the immediate sense of the object contemplated, independent of any faith, or hope that might be entertained as to their ulterior tendency."[22] Stevens also rejects both religion and art as mediators between man and the natural world. To express truly a world of objects, the poet must discover images that are not man-made but are "parts of a world." Neither a harmonium nor a blue guitar will suffice; the titles of the last three books indicate a shift of emphasis from the artificial to the natural: *Transport to Summer, The Auroras of Autumn, The Rock.* By making the actual world his image of man, Stevens will find his own permanence in the cycle of the seasons:

Postpone the anatomy of summer, as
The physical pine, the metaphysical pine.
Let's see the very thing and nothing else.
Let's see it with the hottest fire of sight.
Burn everything not part of it to ash.

Trace the gold sun about the whitened sky
Without evasion by a single metaphor.
Look at it in its essential barrenness
And say this, this is the centre that I seek.
Fix it in an eternal foliage

And fill the foliage with arrested peace,
Joy of such permanence, right ignorance
Of change still possible. Exile desire

For what is not. This is the barrenness
Of the fertile thing that can attain no more.   (CP, 373)

The fixity Stevens sought and could not find in the statue
is now located in "eternal foliage" and a religion of the
particular is celebrated. Seeing is believing, or, as Si-
mone Weil said, absolute attention is prayer ("L'attention absolument sans mélange est prière.") [23] The last
appearance of the statue in Stevens' poetry occurs in
"Things of August" (CP, 489–96)—and a revealing one
it is. Beyond love and hate, beyond good and evil, and
"without desire," the poet is content to be surrounded
by warm colors,

> in the Mediterranean
> Of the quiet of the middle of the night,
> With the broken statues standing on the shore.

The failure of the image was not, however, critical
because the search for permanence which led Stevens
to the statue was simultaneously leading him to its source
material, the rock itself. Just as the poet wished to see
the earth "without evasion by a single metaphor," so he
relentlessly pursued the first cause of art. As an analogy,
the rock was far more effective since it represents a
permanence *in* nature ("The rock cannot be broken. It
is the truth" [CP, 375]); and yet it is involved intimately
in the timely changes occurring in its surroundings.
Vines, leaves, light, and the sea may alter its appearance, just as metaphor disguises fact, but it remains underneath the pure and immutable stone, unshaped by
man, and it is on this rock that Stevens builds his church.
It is not the Christian metaphor for divine order and assurance; it is only itself. Just as the statue serves as the

controlling image for his longest poem, *Owl's Clover*, the rock serves to unify Stevens' last sequence of poems in the *Collected Poems*.

The first appearance of the rock image, however, appears long before "The Rock"; it occurs casually in the final line of "The Bird with the Coppery, Keen Claws" (CP, 82), from *Harmonium*. It is a prophetic use because the poem, nonsensical as it may appear, is a consideration of the permanence-change conflict, a playful answer to a serious metaphysical problem: is there a prime mover, and if so how does he operate in relation to man?

> Above the forest of the parakeets,
> A parakeet of parakeets prevails,
> A pip of life amid a mort of tails.
> . . . .
> His lids are white because his eyes are blind.

This parody of the Lord of Lord's phraseology (with suggestions of "Paraclete") leads Stevens to a characterization of the power behind the shifting forms of natural life. The parakeet god is blind [24] and silent; although he is visible in his natural guise (his "green-vented forms") and ordains the activities on earth, he himself is coldly indifferent to his subjects:

> But though the turbulent tinges undulate
> As his pure intellect applies its laws,
> He moves not on his coppery, keen claws.
>
> He munches a dry shell while he exerts
> His will, yet never ceases, perfect cock,
> To flare, in the sun-pallor of his rock.

Even accepting this initial use of the rock image as fortuitous, or simply dictated by rhyme, it is nevertheless

characteristic of the poet's later linking of the image
with that permanent force in nature which can be observed but never understood or mastered. The rock is
what remains, what the poet must come back to after
his excursions into the realm of the man-made, the
metaphoric.

The rock is both a "rock of summer" (CP, 375) and a
"rock of autumn" (CP, 476); it is that pervasive and timeless unity that Stevens finds behind all natural and human activity. Always tentative in his questions about
man's existence and relative in his answers, Stevens is
wary of statements about truth. As he indicated in his
use of the statue image, the truth cannot be embodied or
fixed. ("The idols have seen lots of poverty,/ Snakes
and gold and lice,/ But not the truth" [CP, 204].) However, having divested stone of its human modifications,
Stevens makes it his only satisfying image of ultimate
meaning. It is that permanence the statue failed to convey, and it is first described in "Credences of Summer"
(CP, 372–78):

> The rock cannot be broken. It is the truth.
> It rises from land and sea and covers them.
> It is a mountain half way green and then,
> The other immeasurable half, such rock
> As placid air becomes. But it is not
>
> A hermit's truth nor symbol in hermitage.
> It is the visible rock, the audible,
> The brilliant mercy of a sure repose,
> On this present ground, the vividest repose,
> Things certain sustaining us in certainty.

The rock exists both in reality ("half way green") and
outside of it ("the other immeasurable half"). It is also

"half way in bloom," hence we find that we can perceive through our senses only the actual; what remains beyond is intensely bright, too dazzling for man's inferior vision. The repose that the rock offers the weary poet is "vivid"; and "vivid sleep" will end the final poem of *The Rock*. The rock is not an artifact like Keats's urn or Eliot's Chinese jar or Stevens' own jar in Tennessee; neither does the image bear, as in Yeats, connotations of mental inflexibility and emotional sterility.[25]

Although the poet continually attempts to get beyond the rock to its source, just as he found in the rock the source material of the statue, he is never successful. To proceed beyond the created would lead into mysticism, where Stevens refuses to go. The couple in "How to Live. What to Do" (CP, 125–26) leave the "flame-freaked sun/ To seek a sun of fuller fire," trying to discover at last the metaphysical meaning of fire, of life itself:

> Instead there was this tufted rock
> Massively rising high and bare
> Beyond all trees, the ridges thrown
> Like great arms among the clouds.
>
> There was neither voice nor created image,
> No chorister, nor priest. There was
> Only the great height of the rock
> And the two of them standing still to rest.

In numerous other poems that follow, Stevens will devise fictive coverings for the rock (and for the stone, a variant image) and momentarily the dress disguises the hard, naked fact underneath. "Slowly the ivy on the stones/ Becomes the stones"—but only in the imagination. The rock, like the sea image, is that impenetrable mystery that man continues to oppose. Ahab would have *the* truth in a world of possible truths, and he passionately defies the mystery. Stevens is far more resigned and stoical. He lacks satanic energy.

But this is not to say that Stevens is apathetic. While accepting man's limitations, he works at understanding them. Like Camus' Sisyphus,[26] he accepts absurdity, and yet the futility of overcoming his rock does not engender despair. The poet may undergo dark moments, when the rock of existence is hard to bear, as in "The Man With the Blue Guitar":

> The earth is not earth but a stone,
> Not the mother that held men as they fell
>
> But stone, but like a stone, no: not
> The mother, but an oppressor, but like
>
> An oppressor that grudges them their death,
> As it grudges the living that they live.   (CP, 173)

Nevertheless, "The Man With the Blue Guitar" is affirmative, accepting the actual world we cannot transcend, and at the same time welcoming the momentary diversions of the imagination which make our return to the physical more fulfilling. The future may come, but

> Here is its actual stone. The bread
> Will be our bread, the stone will be
>
> Our bed and we shall sleep by night.
> We shall forget by day, except
>
> The moments when we choose to play
> The imagined pine, the imagined jay.   (CP, 184)

Stone is the "inexplicable base" (CP, 185) for all flights of the imagination, and sometimes Stevens, with considerable bravura, tries to deny the existence of crude reality, preferring to relish his own creative force which he feels is equal to the force of nature. For example, in "Jumbo" (CP, 269) the poet sees the wind as a "companion" who is absolutely free of restrictions (like man's imagination) and capable of unlimited self-expression. Imagining himself with this power, the poet enjoys a flight into the "egotistical sublime" where "there are no rocks/ And stones, only this imager." Normally, however, Stevens cannot fully imagine away the world of "things." The stone may become a "bouquet" (CP, 227) in the mind's eye, but it can never be eliminated, only lightened or softened, as in "An Ordinary Evening in New Haven":

the shadow of bare rock,

Becomes the rock of autumn, glittering,
Ponderable source of each imponderable,
The weight we lift with the finger of a dream,

The heaviness we lighten by light will,
By the hand of desire, faint, sensitive, the soft
Touch and trouble of the touch of the actual hand.
    (CP, 476)

Knowledge that the hand, like the rock, is "actual" unites the observer, in the only possible way, with the source of life. Reason can never effect such a marriage because it aims at establishing categories and distinguishing identities. Only the "willed dream," which is another name for the imagination, can comfort man when he is faced with the rock of existence.

In the three poems from the *Collected Poems* called
"The Rock," Stevens brings to a close his search for an
image of permanence, but the answer he discovers is
not new: it was inherent in *Harmonium.* The god of the
parakeets "in the sun-pallor of his rock" is now recognized as Stevens' God — a blind, relentless, and impersonal force, revealing itself in the changingness it controls. The fictive covering falls away and we find that
Harmonium was not a work of essential gaudiness, only
superficial gaudiness. Underneath the nonsense, the
comic mannerisms, the "tink and tank and tunk-a-tunk-
tunk," was the rock which Stevens glorifies because it
has no church, interprets because it has no voice. "I
wish that I might be a thinking stone," said the speaker
in "Le Monocle de Mon Oncle." And in these serious
(but not solemn) last poems, Stevens has become the
voice of the rock and of the night, a celebrant of his own
mortality.

The first poem is a farewell to his life and his art,
which is now seen as illusion,

> an illusion so desired

> That the green leaves came and covered the high rock.
>   (CP, 526)

But the green leaves still cover the rock in their season,
just as man's imagination ("the fiction of the leaves")
disguises and softens the fact of death in his season.
Man's form is, then, another "particular of being," and
because he is always *becoming,* the past with all its
achievements, comforts and losses, is that which never
was.

The second poem would likewise appear to deny the
sufficiency of the health poetry can insure. Stevens had

said, in "Esthétique du Mal," that he could not abide
the traditional God:

> A too, too human god, self-pity's kin
> And uncourageous genesis . . . It seems
> As if the health of the world might be enough.
>   (CP, 315)

His tentative *as if* underscores his need for more than
the bare reality of the planet. Now he realizes that he
must be cured of the need for certainty, the illusory
satisfactions that art provides:

> It is not enough to cover the rock with leaves.
> We must be cured of it by a cure of the ground
> Or a cure of ourselves, that is equal to a cure
>
> Of the ground . . .   (CP, 526)

The cure for man's alienation on his own planet, and of
his anxiety before the ineffable, turns out to be the very
poetry he doubts. But it is not a poetry of disguise, illusion, or escape; it is a poetry that helps man look
deeply into himself, realizing that his achievements are
as transient as the leaves, yet as perennial. Poetry is a
fiction, but we give ourselves to it *knowing* it is a fiction.
Thus art becomes a means of knowledge, but subordinate to the life it illuminates. The tentative *if* and *might
be* of the opening stanzas of "The Rock" are shortly
replaced by direct, positive statement. Natural process,
like the poetic process, makes the barren rock fruitful,
by supplying the leaves that deny its lifelessness:

>   these cover the rock.
> These leaves are the poem, the icon and the man.
>   (CP, 527)

Stevens' use of "icon" is a last, residual lingering of
the image of the statue, and the separation of art and nature which it suggested. The icon, with its connotations
of past history and the permanence of art that Yeats represented in Byzantium, has lost all of its artificial characteristics. It is swamped by the luxuriant world. By a
series of equations, Stevens produces a world of harmony in which his four figures (leaves, poem, icon, and
man) are identified individually with each other. The
poem becomes a religious object and an art object, but
it is also man himself and the physical world in which he
moves. All of this proliferation of the "icon" gives the
"statue" life, and it is undertaken "in the predicate that
there is nothing else."

That the rock can be barren, that life can be stark poverty, is a possibility that Stevens entertains but cannot
finally accept—because there is man, and as long as he
exists we will have poems and "the poem makes meanings of the rock." (Stevens, of course, does not restrict
himself to poetry *qua* poetry; like Faulkner, he means
man's voice, singing out until the "last ding-dong of
doom.") If we see the rock as the ineffable truth that
men call God, we discover that Stevens' poetry is aimed
at articulating the power that is within nature:

> In this plenty, the poem makes meanings of the rock,
> Of such mixed motion and such imagery
> That its barrenness becomes a thousand things
>
> And so exists no more. This is the cure
> Of leaves and of the ground and of ourselves.
> His words are both the icon and the man.   (CP, 527)

These closing lines are similar to others that can be read
as a denial of any power outside man. They could, how-

ever, be read in another way.[27] The barrenness of the
rock is so altered by the human will and imagination
that its meanings are fructified in expression and hence
the *barrenness,* and not the rock itself, exists no longer.
The meanings are "mixed," but the rock is absolutely
singular. ("The lord whose oracle is at Delphi neither
speaks nor conceals, but gives signs," said Heraclitus.)
God exists no more as pure idea, neither as statue nor
rock resting on the barrenness of fact; He is redeemed
by the human imagination and now resides in man. This
knowledge is the cure. And it is Stevens' affirmation of
creative life and the power that is housed in nature that
makes him, in a Wordsworthian sense, religious. Like
Wordsworth, "his theme is nature *in solido,* that is to
say, he dwells on that mysterious presence of surrounding things, which imposes itself on any separate element
which we set up as an individual for its own sake." [28]
Stevens was speaking of "nobility" when he wrote the
following, but would we go wrong in wondering whether
what he is in effect defining—rather *not* defining—is
God?

I mean that nobility which is our spiritual height and depth;
and while I know how difficult it is to express it, nevertheless
I am bound to give a sense of it. Nothing could be more eva-
sive and inaccessible. Nothing distorts itself and seeks disguise more quickly. There is a shame of disclosing it and in its
definite presentations a horror of it. But there it is. The fact
that it is there is what makes it possible to invite to the reading and writing of poetry men of intelligence and desire for
life. I am not thinking of the ethical or the sonorous or at all
of the manner of it. The manner of it is, in fact, its difficulty,
which each man must feel each day differently, for himself.
I am not thinking of the solemn, the portentous or demoded.
On the other hand, I am evading a definition. If it is defined,

it will be fixed and it must not be fixed. As is the case of an external thing, nobility resolves itself into an enormous number of vibrations, movements, changes. To fix it is to put an end to it. Let me show it to you unfixed.   (NA, 33–34)

In the last poem from "The Rock," Stevens achieves a serene and beatific state, in which he comprehends the rock in all its conditions: by day, by night, and in "the difficult rightness of half-risen day." (The acceptance of uncertainty, of half-knowledge, as man's burden is contained in this apt phrase.) The rock is the beginning and the end of life: "origin of the mango's rind" and "the starting point of the human and the end." And it is the "habitation of the whole," that unity of being that Stevens labored all his life to find.

In section VI of "It Must Change" (CP, 389–98), of *Notes toward a Supreme Fiction*, for example, the poet had realized that there was "a single text, granite monotony," a permanence which man and bird attempted to deny in their individual ways. Each "bethou me" of each bird was an expression of man's desire to achieve the permanence which he celebrates in song but cannot find through labors of the mind:

> These are of minstrels lacking minstrelsy,
> Of an earth in which the first leaf is the tale
> Of leaves, in which the sparrow is a bird
>
> Of stone, that never changes. Bethou him, you
> And you, bethou him and bethou. It is
> A sound like any other. It will end.   (CP, 394)

Art, Stevens implies, is an ephemeral version of that "single text."

Stevens faces the same unhappy separation of singer and song at the end of "The Rock," but a union is achieved. The title of the poem is "Forms of the Rock in a Night-Hymn" (CP, 528), which announces that the Night-Hymn (the poem, the human utterance) is distinct from the rock (the reality man expresses). The rock is simply praised by "man's eye" which is a "silent rhapsodist" ("There is no place,/ Here, for the lark fixed in the mind,/ In the museum of the sky" [CP, 182]). By the time we reach the final line, however, a transformation has taken place. The poem opens with "The rock is the gray particular of man's life," emphasizing man, his aspirations, his ends. But the poem closes without reference to man or his problems. A slight verbal change is the clue to a profound acceptance of man's limitations. The man-artist has been transmuted into the object of his contemplation, the voice of his universe:

> That in which space itself is contained, the gate
> To the enclosure, day, the things illumined
>
> By day, night and that which night illumines,
> Night and its midnight-minting fragrances,
> Night's hymn of the rock, as in a vivid sleep.

The "Night-Hymn" has become "Night's hymn" and the poet has found his consummation by surrendering himself to the earth he could not finally accept as a statue — or imagine away. Wordsworth records in "Tintern Abbey" such a moment when

> we are laid asleep
> In body, and become a living soul:
> While with an eye made quiet by the power

> Of harmony, and the deep power of joy,
> We see into the life of things.

The eye must be quiet, and it is of the greatest importance that we do not see *things* but the *life* of things. The
image of the rock was finally what led Stevens not to
"the symbol but that for which the symbol stands" (CP,
238).

5 COLORS AND "DOMINATION OF BLACK"

"After all, they knew that to be
real each had
To find for himself his earth,
his sky, his sea.

And the words for them and the
colors that they possessed."

Holiday in Reality

Because Stevens links the sun with human creative power, he finds in the various shifting colors of the world the surest analogue of the imaginative process. Colors are therefore often used, for the want of a better word, symbolically,[1] not limited solely to actual perception, although based initially on observation. There is no split between image and meaning, no explanatory matter or iconography by which the color symbols are made understandable. The only way to define, say, "green" at any one point is to study all the other uses of the color, in its differing contexts. "A symbol," George Kane wrote, "does not discard its earlier sense; it simply adds a new one to this, and although the new meaning is uppermost for the moment, it soon merges with the previous senses to the enrichment of the symbol." [2] This is not to say that Stevens never speaks literally of "blue" skies and

"green" plants; rather, that he refuses to be restricted
to simple nominal terms, stripped of their valuable associations or overtones. No pure colors exist. Like a painter,
Stevens enjoys the endless variations that light makes
on solid surfaces, the effect of one color on another. As
Malraux said of Cézanne,

He paints the Montagne Sainte-Victoire again and again not
because he does not find his picture sufficiently "true to life"
but because at certain moments the mountain conjures up new
color schemes, implementing a fuller "realization"; it is not
the mountain he wants to "realize" but the picture.[3]

To say, as William York Tindall does, that Stevens
uses colors as intellectual counters whose meanings
are fixed [4] is to contradict a central Stevens' belief, long
ago indicated by Robert Pack, that "having shown how
an emotion is misunderstood when seen in isolation, he
goes on to show us how an idea is abused when held to
the exclusion of other ideas." [5] Unlike Eliot, whose use
of color is sparing and almost exclusively allegorical,
Stevens has no base of dogma, no system of thought that
his colors can exemplify. The natural world is the origin
of all of his ideas; hence color is both the exterior effects
of light as well as the interior resources of the imagination. The absence of color is in Stevens a metaphor for
death (actual or imaginative) whereas in Eliot it may reveal a desire to transcend the physical world.

In an account of a return to the country of his Dutch
ancestors in Pennsylvania (NA, 101–02), Stevens described the bleached colors of the sheep in the fields,
as well as the abandoned church, equally colorless, "the
upper part of each window white with the half-drawn
blind, the lower part black with the vacantness of space."

He was faced with the "vacant" reality of the place and the "desolation that penetrated like something final." After returning to New York, the "color" of some books of tales, of poetry and folklore, gave, he found, "illumination" and vitality to the cold, barren, colorless scene he had experienced. In contrast, the abandoned church of Little Gidding, the colorless abstractions it evokes, helps Eliot the poet realize his own need to escape the ephemeral, to "put off/ Sense" and seek "detachment/ From self and from things and from persons." The thoroughgoing distinction between the two poets is that Stevens' "hedonism" conceives a "reality" that is intolerable without both literal and imaginative color; Eliot's "puritanism" leads to a rejection of the earth's colorful surfaces, and the imagination's celebrations, in the interest of cultivating a higher "reality." For example, of the five colors appearing in the *Four Quartets* — red, brown, white, black, and gray — only three are properly colors at all, and the brown and red are employed negatively: The dry, concrete pool is "brown edged" and the hollyhocks in the garden are decaying, "red into grey." We cannot dismiss completely Havelock Ellis's overstated remark that "when we have ascertained a writer's colour formula and his colours of predilection, we can tell at a glance, simply and reliably, something about his view of the world which pages of description could only tell us with uncertainty." [6]

Albert William Levi's accurate description of the differing approaches of Stevens and Eliot to color is symptomatic of a much deeper separation of world-views:

The adjective in Stevens is a device of presentational immediacy, used for the pictorial representation of surface quality. But the adjective in Eliot is used allegorically, for the elucidation of meanings which transcend surface appearances. The violet is the violet of penance. The green is the green of hope. The white is the white of purity. The blue is the blue of heaven. Even the sensory vividness of color is used in the service of symbolic reference.[7]

The word "allegory" is significant here, because of Stevens' reservations about this literary mode. It was for him a mode in danger of becoming solely a mental exercise, arbitrary and stultifying. For him, *Pilgrim's Progress* was more or less a failure because its allegorical equivalents were too mathematically exact, leaving no room for the free play of the emotions and the imagination.[8] Even his praise of *The Faerie Queene* is not for its intellectual structure but for Spenser's ability to create a work "charged throughout with the *emotions* of the poet" (NA, 112). (My italics.) The poem is a great work because it triumphs over the artificiality of allegory and "creates a sensibility."

For Stevens, systems of thought are deadening because "nature is not mechanical" (NA, 73). Each color may resemble another, as each man resembles another, but to attempt to limit the individual emotional effects of color is to limit our knowledge of the world.[9] Again like a painter, Stevens uses color as a means of knowledge not translatable into verbal signs, unless the signs remain flexible.[10] In using color words to suggest emotions, releasing them from the restrictions of a conscious allegory, he hopes to enlarge our appreciation of the world, or as he said of Spenser to create "a sensibility." He would probably agree with Ogden and Richards that "the elementary signs of language are only 26 letters. If out of these 26 letters we can get the whole of literature and science, the 250,000 optic nerve fibres can be relied

on for an even richer and more finely graded knowledge." [11]

We should attempt to find in Stevens' use of colors,
then, a pattern of emotional association, but no rigid intellectual one. Although we may find numerous – and
sometimes even contradictory – significances for his
symbols, the poet warns the reader in his essay "Effects
of Analogy" (NA, 107–30) not to be "distracted" by
meanings to the extent that he forgets the concrete world
from which the symbol draws its life. Writing of the
superiority of the *Fables* of La Fontaine to *Pilgrim's
Progress*, Stevens could as well be speaking of his own
color symbolism:

> Our attention is on the symbol, which is interesting in itself.
> The other meaning does not dog the symbol like its shadow.
> It is not attached to it. Here the effect of analogy almost ceases
> to exist and the reason for this is, of course, that we are not
> particularly conscious of it. We do not have to stand up and
> take it. It is like a play of thought, some trophy that we our-
> selves gather, some meaning that we ourselves supply. It is
> like a pleasant shadow, faint and volatile.   (NA, 109)

After looking at a few poems that display Stevens' general use of color, I shall discuss some individual colors,
concentrating largely on blue and green, which continue
the series of polarities or antithetical images discussed
in previous chapters.

In "Cy Est Pourtraicte, Madame Ste Ursule, et Les
Unze Mille Vierges" (CP, 21–22) Stevens creates a poem
that has nothing to do with the legendary tale of the
martyrdom of ten thousand virgins by the pagans.
Several versions of the tale exist. In one ancient one,
Ursula the daughter of a Christian king of Britain is

betrothed to the son of a pagan king, but she delays the
marriage by a journey with her virgin companions, ending in death at the hands of the Huns. As usual with
Stevens, history or myth provides a referent but not a
subject. The pattern of color imagery, and not medieval
legend, is the key to the poem.

Ursula, like Eve or Persephone, is found in the garden, surrounded by flowers. Innocent, she is the creature of nature, her offering a celebration of the physical
world:

> She dressed in red and gold brocade
> And in the grass an offering made
> Of radishes and flowers.

In the picture there is a noticeable lack of virginal white
or ascetic gray, no suggestion of Christian denial or
renunciation. She creates a natural ceremony, enjoying
the material "red and gold brocade" that links her with
the sun.[12]

In direct contrast, her offering to the Lord of nature —
not the Lord in nature — is more refined, removed from
the world of green grass and common radishes:

> She said, "My dear,
> Upon your altars,
> I have placed
> The marguerite and coquelicot,
> And roses
> Frail as April snow . . .

The delicacy and femininity of this offering (the French
names, the white marguerite) is further reinforced by
the poem's only simile, introducing suggestions of cold
chastity. Ursula's conflict is one that Stevens often pre-

sents: which to prefer, the purity of the mind or the sensory delights of the physical world, the metaphysical or the physical God. Stevens' God makes no judgment, neither does he respond; he simply continues his creation:

> The good Lord in His garden sought
> New leaf and shadowy tinct . . .

God is not a thing apart from the world, passively waiting to be glorified; he seeks further creation, "new" leaves and fresh "tinct." Stevens here, as in other poems, parallels divine and artistic creation. God and the poet delight in and celebrate the physical world while continuing to enlarge it, to find new colors. The natural altar seems to serve God more appropriately than the artificial one. Art is not artifice, in the sense that artificial contrasts with natural; art is more collaboration than imitation, for, as Jacques Maritain writes,

. . . if it is true that art is a creative virtue of the intellect, which tends to engender in beauty, and that it catches hold, in the created world, of the secret workings of nature in order to produce its own work — a new creature — the consequence is that art continues in its own way the labor of divine creation.[13]

Since color is not intrinsic to objects, but is created by light waves *and* the observer's eye, the actual sun and the sun of the imagination, Stevens often dramatizes the changing effects of color on the "solid, static objects extended in space" (NA, 31) which is for him the world without imagination. In "Of Hartford in a Purple Light" (CP, 226–27), he contrasts the various changes that light makes on the city's surfaces, the quickening effect it has on the "aunts in Pasadena" who by imagining the lively light begin to "abhor the plaster of the western horses,/ Souvenirs of museums." The souvenir horses are an occurrence of the "statue" image, dead form removed from the light's transformations. The poem ends by naturalizing the city, much as Wordsworth did in his sonnet "Composed Upon Westminster Bridge":

>   Look, Master,
> See the river, the railroad, the cathedral . . .
>
> When male light fell on the naked back
> Of the town, the river, the railroad were clear.
> Now, every muscle slops away.
>
> Hi! whisk it, poodle, flick the spray
> Of the ocean, ever-freshening,
> On the irised hunks, the stone bouquet.

Whereas Wordsworth's London is made tolerable by the absence of human activity, Stevens' Hartford is made energetic by light and color. But in neither case is the city like Baudelaire's (and Eliot's) "unreal city." In Wordsworth:

> This City now doth, like a garment, wear
> The beauty of the morning; silent, bare,
> Ships, towers, domes, theatres, and temples lie
> Open unto the fields, and to the sky . . .

By stopping momentarily the pulse of the great city, silencing its clamor, Wordsworth transforms it into a natural object fit for contemplation. And Stevens, likewise, effects a metamorphosis of the man-made into the natural: the bodies of buildings are muscular in the masculine light, in the feminine light the hunks of buildings become irises, the stones a bouquet.

The "solid, static objects extended in space" compose a dead world that is resurrected each day by the sun-imagination. In "Attempt to Discover Life" (CP, 370), we encounter two death figures — a "cadaverous" man and a "pallid-skinned" woman — who are seeking the meaning of life in a cafe in San Miguel de los Baños. Like vampires, or like Coleridge's life-in-death image in "The Rime of the Ancient Mariner," the two colorless creatures invade the southern scene where

> The waitress heaped up black Hermosas
> In the magnificence of a volcano.
> Round them she spilled the roses
> Of the place, blue and green, both streaked,
> And white roses shaded emerald on petals
> Out of the deadliest heat.

The exotic Hermosas (a variety of roses) are juxtaposed with the local roses, and they produce a warm feast of imaginary colors. Roses are neither black nor blue nor green, and yet the human imagination can create, rather than imitate, the things of nature, as Cézanne created blue forms to replace actual cypresses.[14] Stevens' colors, whether imaginary or real, are capable of purging the scene of death. The atmosphere of the cafe in San Miguel de los Baños is bathed in radiant colors, one dynamically shifting into another or evolving into smoke:

> The green roses drifted up from the table
> In smoke. The blue petals became
> The yellowing fomentations of effulgence,

Among fomentations of black bloom and of white bloom.
The cadaverous persons were dispelled.
On the table near which they stood
Two coins were lying—dos centavos.

Color, the poem obliquely says, is the meaning of life,
knowledge is the realization of the vivid, amorphous,
and self-consuming fire of both the imagination and
reality. What remains? The fact of the two coins survives
the fiction of the flowers, the artifice of the arranged
"volcano." We are again, as often with Stevens, left with
the lesson that living precedes all questions about the
value of life. Life, indeed, may be worth only two cents.
Its colorful surface is all that is knowable.

Just as color dispels the death figures, the absence of
vital color can often produce in Stevens a state of depression or despair which is a kind of death. Contemplating the austere monotony of a neighborhood of
"white night-gowns" in "Disillusionment of Ten
O'Clock" (CP, 66), the poet laments the lack of individual response to life, the passionless conformity which
drains the color from any experience. Color becomes a
metaphor for the imagination and emotion lacking in
the bloodless ghosts [15] that men become when they deny
their potentialities:

> None are green,
> Or purple with green rings,
> Or green with yellow rings,
> Or yellow with blue rings.

This piling-up of colors serves no systematic symbolism;
rather, it represents the variety of possibilities afforded

by a rich imagination. Stevens not only believes "the eccentric to be the base of design" (CP, 151) but also finds in outrageously colorful dress man's kinship with ostentatious nature.[16] In "Credences of Summer" (CP, 372–78), for example, although God does not communicate with the characters he creates, he does observe

> Them mottled, in the moodiest costumes,
>
> Of blue and yellow, sky and sun, belted
> And knotted, sashed and seamed, half pales of red,
> Half pales of green, appropriate habit for
> The huge decorum, the manner of the time,
> Part of the mottled mood of summer's whole . . .

"Disillusionment of Ten O'Clock" ends affirmatively, with at least one person capable of imaginative vision:

> Only, here and there, an old sailor,
> Drunk and asleep in his boots,
> Catches tigers
> In red weather.

Only the drunkard, the irrational man ("Poetry must be irrational" [OP, 162]), who is in touch with the unconscious—represented here, and often elsewhere, by the sea—can awake his own passionate nature until his blood is mirrored in the very weather. The theme occurs in a number of romantic and symbolist poems.[17] The symbolists, particularly, were fascinated with drunkenness as a trope for the imaginative life, freed from the restrictions of bourgeois thinking. Baudelaire's "Le Voyage" is remarkably close to Stevens, although Baudelaire does not exploit color imagery:

O le pauvre amoureux des pays chimériques!
Faut-il le mettre aux fers, le jeter à la mer,
Ce matelot ivrogne, inventeur d'Amériques
Dont le mirage rend la gouffre plus amer?

Tel le vieux, vagabond, piétinant dans la boue,
Reve, le nez en l'air, de brillants paradis;
Son oeil ensorcelé découvre une Capoue
Partout où la chandelle illumine un taudis.

Unlike Mallarmé, neither Stevens nor Baudelaire ignores the matter-of-fact world, but the poets differ in that Baudelaire would transcend it, Stevens would transform it. Colors are almost continuously absent from Baudelaire's world: His pervasive color is black, indicating, perhaps, that he wishes to escape the colorful world of natural process. In contrast, Stevens believes that the poet "creates the world to which we turn incessantly" (NA, 31). Although he sees his role as a spiritual one, he declares that the true poet, alone, "does not turn to Paris or Rome for relief from the monotony of reality. He turns to himself, and he denies that reality was ever monotonous except in comparison" (OP, 213). At times, Stevens somewhat resembles Swift's fat spider in *The Battle of The Books* whose large castle, he says, is "all built with my own hands, and the material extracted altogether out of my own person." Rejecting as he does both the past and the community of knowledge, Stevens seeks to discover his "sweetness and light" through exploitation of the self. Like the sun, the poet must engender himself:

The sun is seeking something bright to shine on.
The trees are wooden, the grass is yellow and thin.
The ponds are not the surfaces it seeks.
It must create its colors out of itself.   (CP, 157–58)

Here is the romantic limitation which Swift foretold and Eliot attempted to overcome through his "continual extinction of personality."

The dominant colors in Stevens' palette arc blue and green. Both appear the same number of times in his work — 163, exclusive of combinations such as leaf-green, blue-shadowed, etc. — and far outnumber uses of other colors — red 85; yellow 43; brown 18. Stevens' use of the two colors amplifies the opposition of imagination and reality already displayed through the juxtaposition of other images (e.g., north-south). Blue, the color of the sky, the traditional image of "heavenly Creation" and "divine wisdom" [18] is associated with the imagination; green is Dylan Thomas's "force that through the green fuse drives the flower," the *élan vital* of nature, the reality outside the mind which in its "chaos and barbarism" has the potential both to replenish and to engulf any order created by "bluest reason" (CP, 124).

Stevens' obsession with blue and green points to a concern with the natural world which Havelock Ellis thought characteristic chiefly of "romantic" poets, or poets since the eighteenth century:

The predominance of green and blue — the colours of vegetation, the sky, and the sea — means that the poet is predominantly a poet of nature. If red and its synonyms are supreme, we may assume an absorbing interest in man and woman, for there are the colours of blood and love. . . . And where there is a predominance of black, white and possibly yellow . . . there we shall find that the poet is singing with, as it were, closed eyes, intent on his own inner vision.[19]

Ellis asserts that green is the color "most popular with poets" and that Wordsworth uses green "twice as fre-

quently as any other colour, usually as the almost mechanical attribute of the things he most cares for. . . ." [20]
The psychologist feels that, since red was Shakespeare's
favorite color, romantic poets have turned away from
human relations in the interest of cultivating a relation
with external nature. Regardless of the validity of this
judgment, it seems certain that green has been the color
of natural life and of physical sensation from *The Song
of Songs* through Keats to Dylan Thomas ("Time left me
green and dying").

Stevens uses green in a similar way, contrasted with
the blue of reason or the white of the realm of pure
platonic ideas. In "The Apostrophe to Vincentine"
(CP, 52–53) the speaker is a speculative man who seeks
the rarified "nameless" Vincentine in order to resolve
the eternal conflict between "monotonous earth and
dark blue sky." But he finds that by being idealized the
actual woman becomes colorless, "small and lean."
The first stanza begins "I figured," but by the second
stanza the speaker is down to earth, using his senses:

> I saw you then, as warm as flesh,
> Brunette,
> But yet not too brunette,
> As warm, as clean.
> Your dress was green,
> Was whited green,
> Green Vincentine.

The green of physical contact is experienced, slightly
tinged with the desired ideal: the green is whited. But
the speaker has chosen the actual woman over the ideal,
and the striking effect is that the "heavenly" becomes
the earthly; feeling, not thought, transforms the impoverished and lean earth into a paradise:

> And what I knew you felt
> Came then.
> Monotonous earth I saw become
> Illimitable spheres of you,
> And that white animal, so lean,
> Turned Vincentine,
> Turned heavenly Vincentine,
> And that white animal, so lean,
> Turned heavenly, heavenly Vincentine.

The use of "heavenly" is playfully ironic, since the white ideal has turned earthly green, and what one sees and feels becomes "ideal." The imagination rescues us from an earth that would otherwise be "monotonous."

One would expect to find that Stevens' conception of the Garden of Eden involves the color green, since it so often suggests spontaneous or primitive feelings, unhampered by the strictures of the rational mind.[21] The freedom — both of and from mind — that natural creatures share, their harmony with their environment, is the "green freedom of a cockadoo." Stevens inverts Descartes' "I think therefore I am," so that Part IV, "It Must Be Abstract" (CP, 380–89), of *Notes toward a Supreme Fiction* begins: *t*

> The first idea was not our own. Adam
> In Eden was the father of Descartes
> And Eve made air the mirror of herself,
>
> Of her sons and of her daughters. They found themselves
> In heaven as in a glass; a second earth;
> And in the earth itself they found a green —
>
> The inhabitants of a very varnished green.   (CP, 383)

Eve was the first artist, perhaps, but not the first philosopher: she *made* air the mirror of herself, but she did not attempt to convert natural phenomena into concepts. (Until Satan turned her into a philosopher and consequently brought about her fall.) She experiences that serene passion Marvell found in his garden where "no white nor red was ever seen/ So amorous as this lovely green." [22] And like Narcissus she finds her own image in the external world, thereby intensifying her enjoyment of living: the green is "varnished"; it possesses the "glory" or "splendor" that Wordsworth felt transfigured the ordinary world in the minds of the innocent. Stevens persistently praises this innocence which he does not, like Wordsworth, limit to youth. Narcissus was not for Stevens the self-indulgent egotist but simply the sensitive man who seeks to discover in the created world his reason for being.[23] Eve is special only because she is happily at home. The poet's job is to restore man to that condition (to reclaim what Yeats called "radical innocence") whereby he is capable of enjoying his birthright which he has sold for the pottage of religion and philosophy.

The same association of green with the actual world occurs in an often-quoted passage from "Esthétique du Mal":

> The greatest poverty is not to live
> In a physical world, to feel that one's desire
> Is too difficult to tell from despair. Perhaps,
> After death, the non-physical people, in paradise,
> Itself non-physical, may, by chance, observe
> The green corn gleaming and experience
> The minor of what we feel. The adventurer
> In humanity has not conceived of a race
> Completely physical in a physical world.
> The green corn gleams and the metaphysicals
> Lie sprawling in majors of the August heat,
> The rotund emotions, paradise unknown.   (CP, 325)

The paradise here is both unknown and unknowable, and the sensory response to the green corn gleaming is all that is. The difficulty, as with the recollection of Eden in *Notes toward a Supreme Fiction,* is that Stevens is never able to become the completely physical creature that green symbolizes. Like Eve, he hungers for absolute knowledge. Since the myth of the Garden is no longer active in Hartford, and since the "metaphysicals" refuse to be ignored, the poet lives in a tension out of which all his poems grow. Stevens put his dilemma clearly when he wrote in *Notes toward a Supreme Fiction:*

> From this the poem springs: that we live in a place
> That is not our own and, much more, not ourselves
> And hard it is in spite of blazoned days.   (CP, 383)

Susanna, in "Peter Quince at the Clavier," is a part of a paradisiac "green evening," bathing in "green water," an integral part of natural process and its "green going." But she is shocked from her harmony by the "red-eyed elders." Both the idea of an absolute and the force of human passion are violences that prevent Stevens from sharing Marvell's tranquil green.

"Sea Surface Full of Clouds," discussed earlier in connection with the sea, is a piece of virtuosity that demonstrates an adage of Stevens: "The proliferation of resemblances extends an object" (NA, 78). Just as Eve made the air a "mirror of herself," Stevens indulges his desire to refresh the world, to recover a spontaneity lost through excessive intellection. The poet chooses as his object the moving sea on which appear moving clouds, both of which are kept in further motion by the imagination, which creates new forms out of the myriad forms of nature. The odd and unexpected — almost surrealistic — resemblances perceived by the poet are like those resulting from a Rorschach test: the test images in reality are forms, but the imagination of man can convert them into what he chooses, bringing into question the very nature of "reality." [24] The recurrent resemblances that unify the poem, besides a French refrain contained in each section, are chocolate, umbrellas, machine, and the colors blue and green. The poem displays both the penetrating and the transforming power of the imagination, a subject amplified by Stevens in an essay:

It is as if a man who lived indoors should go outdoors on a day of sympathetic weather. His realization of the weather would exceed that of a man who lives outdoors. It might, in fact, be intense enough to convert the real world about him into an imagined world. In short, a sense of reality keen enough to be in excess of the normal sense of reality creates a reality of its own.   (NA, 79)

The color green can be taken as an illustration of the way the poet effects his transformations. Throughout the poem, until the final section when it becomes an adjective, green is anonymous, having a natural existence but unrelated to man until the poet discovers the modifying adjective which claims it with his personal signature. In an act of imaginative legerdemain, green becomes in turn: paradisal, swimming, sham-like, uncertain, too fluent, thinking, and motley. All of the adjectives, of course, reveal Stevens' personal conception of form in external nature which, in its variety and constantly changing life, mirrors his own mind. Again, Stevens resembles Heraclitus who, as Philip Wheelwright comments, was a man unconditioned by cartesian dualism and for whom "the division between objective and subjective wore no such appearance of clarity and finality.

The idea of what might belong to the one and what might belong to the other would vary according to mood and circumstance, and no precise question about it was ever raised."²⁵

Far from the disillusioned and imaginatively fallow state of "The Plain Sense of Things" (CP, 502–03) where "It is difficult even to choose the adjective/ For this blank cold, this sadness without cause," in "Sea Surface Full of Clouds" Stevens is happily at work, finding the right adjectives, refreshing the old world by redescribing it. The green "reality" remains, but the artist, like the mariners in *The Auroras of Autumn*, makes it new through language:

> It was the same,
> Except for the adjectives, an alteration
> Of words that was a change of nature, more
>
> Than the difference that clouds make over a town.
> The countrymen were changed and each constant thing.
> Their dark-colored words had redescribed the citrons.
>   (CP, 487)

"Sea Surface Full of Clouds" in its play of variations, of which green is but one, is probably as close to Valéry's definition of "pure poetry" as Stevens ever came:

. . . if the poet could manage to construct works in which nothing of prose ever appeared, poems in which the musical continuity was never broken, in which the relations between meanings were themselves perpetually similar to harmonic relations, *in which the transmutation of thoughts into each other appeared more important than any thought,* in which the play of figures contained the reality of the subject—then one could speak of *pure poetry* as of something that existed.²⁶

Stevens' nostalgia for a prelapsarian state has, of
course, nothing to do with the Christian concept of sin
unless we define the term broadly as that which disrupts
the harmony of man and his world, makes him an alien
on his own planet. Sin has been defined as preferring
the created world over the God of creation and by this
definition Stevens is guilty because he cannot make the
separation required. But Stevens' "fall" is primarily
aesthetic, not moral or religious, and it suggests Eliot's
"dissociation of sensibility." [27] Green is the symbol of
that happy state before the "false engagements of the
mind" cut us off from green and "those for whom green
speaks" (CP, 309). Looking at a pineapple, Stevens,
somewhat in the manner of "Sea Surface Full of Clouds,"
attempts to enlarge reality through metaphor. Rejecting
the rationalist's desire to explain the nature of reality,
the poet simply creates twelve "resemblances" which
intensify his enjoyment of his subject:

> There had been an age
> When a pineapple on the table was enough,
>
> Without the forfeit scholar coming in,
> Without his enlargings and pale arrondissements,
> Without the furious roar in his capital.
>
> Green had, those days, its own implacable sting.
>   (NA, 85)

In "those days" — and the "age" is never specified — the
green of reality was actually felt because the scholar's
"pale" explanations, like the "pale intrusions into blue"
(CP, 172) of the player of the "poor pale, poor pale guitar" (CP, 176), had not weakened our response to life.

As we have seen, Stevens suffers the dejection common to romantic poets when they are unable to discover the imagination that balances fact, when fact deposes "the Queen of Fact" ("An Ordinary Evening in New Haven" [CP, 485]). When things are merely things, without the transfiguring fiction that Wordsworth calls "glory," the poet approached despair. "Depression before Spring" (CP, 63) is, despite its nonsensical surface, related in idea to Coleridge's "Dejection: an Ode" and to Wordsworth's "Ode on Intimations of Immortality from Recollections of Early Childhood." The world has somehow lost its freshness.

> The cock crows
> But no queen rises.
>
> The hair of my blonde
> Is dazzling,
> As the spittle of cows
> Threading the wind.
>
> Ho! Ho!
>
> But Ki-ki-ri-ki
> Brings no rou-cou,
> No rou-cou-cou.
>
> But no queen comes
> In slipper green.

The actual cock crows, as it has always done, awakening the poet to the world, announcing a new day and a new season. But the poet's mind is not regenerated: "no queen rises." *Rationally*, he knows that his world is "dazzling" but the imaginative or spiritual response is

inexplicably absent.[28] Stevens wrote that "the greatest
poverty is not to live/ In a physical world" (CP, 325);
however, a "world without imagination" is only half a
world, hence his depression. The final two lines indicate
the consummation the poet seeks: the fusion of imaginative power (queen) with the "green" of reality, the "as-
if" with the "is." The poet seeks to awaken his dormant
imagination, just as he does later in "Description without
Place"

> It was a queen that made it seem
> By the illustrious nothing of her name.
>
> Her green mind made the world around her green.
> The queen is an example . . . This green queen
>
> In the seeming of the summer of her sun
> By her own seeming made the summer change.
>   (CP, 339)

Stevens desires to bring green mind into harmony with
green world because he believes that all knowledge
ends with the physical, that green survives all the
golden classical myths as well as the Christian idea of
heaven. The woman in "Sunday Morning" realizes this,
that there is no idea,

> Neither the golden underground, nor isle
> Melodious, where spirits gat them home,
> Nor visionary south, nor cloudy palm
> Remote on heaven's hill, that has endured
> As April's green endures . . .   (CP, 68)

In one of Stevens' late poems from *The Rock*, "The
Green Plant" (CP, 506), "April's green endures" in the

plant which symbolizes the "harsh reality" which can never be subjugated by the mind. The speaker is stripped of illusions, in the autumn of life, no longer able to break the surrounding silence with his metaphors because

> The effete vocabulary of summer
> No longer says anything.
> The brown at the bottom of red
> The orange far down in yellow.

The earth's colors, the changing, mingling colors that had evoked for the poet all the zestful variety of both actual and imaginative life, are now "falsifications from a sun/ In a mirror, without heat . . . ." The image of psychic and imaginative energy, the sun, no longer operates to renew the poet's body or his poems — both are "turning down toward finality . . . ."

But Stevens does not end his poem on this sad note of loss. To be alive is to change; to perceive change is to be most alive. Like Penelope, in "The World as Meditation," the poet realizes that there is a "barbarous strength within" that continues to survive, and it is associated with green. The poet would enter a state of despair

> Except that a green plant glares, as you look
> At the legend of the maroon and olive forest,
> Glares, outside of the legend, with the barbarous green
> Of the harsh reality of which it is part.

In "The Comedian as the Letter C," Crispin attempted to create a life and an aesthetic that could incorporate this "barbarous" green, but without defining it out of existence. He wished for "an aesthetic tough, diverse, untamed,/ Incredible to prudes, the mint of dirt,/ Green barbarism turned paradigm" (CP, 31). Now in his old age, the poet again declares that Crispin's "paradigm" and his own "legend" (the half-colors, the subtle mixtures of maroon and olive) fail to soften the harsh fact of reality. The poem records a wished-for failure. Because Stevens insists that "sense exceeds all metaphor" (CP, 431), he is content to accept the glare of harsh reality, green's "own implacable sting," knowing that finally "It is the poet's sense of the world that is the poet's world" (NA, 118).

Blue is Stevens' symbol for both reason and the imagination, what Wordsworth called "reason in her most exhalted mood." [29] The color, when it is not being used in a literal, descriptive way, seems always to have suggestions of that human faculty which attempts to unify the disparate colors in external nature. "The poet," Stevens writes, "in order to fulfill himself, must accomplish a poetry that satisfies both the reason and the imagination" (NA, 42). And elsewhere he obviously distinguishes the two: "If, for the poet, the imagination is paramount, and if he dwells apart in his imagination, as the philosopher dwells in his reason, and as the priest dwells in his belief . . ." (NA, 66). But his use of blue in the poetry does not support this conceptual distinction. Reason is blue—"We hardened ourselves to live by bluest reason . . ." (CP, 124)—but "The Man With the Blue Guitar," Stevens' most overt use of blue as symbol, is in the poet's own words a work of "pure imagination." The color is perhaps best characterized as a symbol for speculative thought, or simply for the mind.

In "The Man With the Blue Guitar" Stevens first treats the war between the imagination and reality explicitly in terms of color. Blue is associated with the moon, as it is later referred to as "blue and its deep inversions in the moon" (CP, 309), and with the northern cold in which the poet can be removed from the relentless pressures of the green, physical world. Like the moon, blue is often seen as an evasion; within the "imbecile revery" of the poet, natural colors of buds and blooms can become weakened:

> The pale intrusions into blue
> Are corrupting pallors . . . ay di mi,
>
> Blue buds or pitchy blooms. Be content—
> Expansions, diffusions—content to be
>
> The unspotted imbecile revery,
> The heraldic center of the world
>
> Of blue, blue sleek with a hundred chins,
> The amorist Adjective aflame . . .   (CP, 172) [30]

The juxtaposition of reality's green with the blue of the imagination is clearly made at the beginning of the poem when it is announced that "the day was green" and "things as they are/ Are changed upon the blue guitar." The pervasive paradox of the poem is that the poet wishes to be detached from the physical and yet remain part of it, to play "a tune beyond us as we are." Just as the poet fluctuates between sun and moon, he cannot commit himself totally to either blue or green, to the imagination or to reality.

> Poetry is the subject of the poem,
> From this the poem issues and
>
> To this returns. Between the two,
> Between issue and return, there is

> An absence in reality,
> Things as they are. Or so we say.
>
> But are these separate? Is it
> An absence for the poem, which acquires
>
> Its true appearances there, sun's green,
> Cloud's red, earth feeling, sky that thinks?
>
> From these it takes. Perhaps it gives,
> In the universal intercourse.   (CP, 176–77)

The incessant "intercourse" between imagination and reality that Stevens dramatizes as colors is sometimes temporarily stopped, suspended in the mind, but the armistice is quickly broken by the poet's need to escape the restrictions of thought and return to spontaneous feeling.

Very early in his career, blue began to take on symbolic value. Hi Simons believed that "between 1915 and 1919 he developed 'blue' as a symbol so that, after the latter year, the word always, except when used literally or as a simple metonymy, represents in his work the imagination or something connected with it, such as the romantic or the imaginative in contradistinction to the realistic." [31] For Stevens, man's identity seems equally endangered by submission to either Blake's "mind-forged manacles" or his "Tyger" of wild emotions. The "harsh" or "barbarous" green is not happily replaced by a blue that can be "cold" and, in its own way, equally "savage." Blue as a primary color, fixed, clearly unified, uncorrupted by other colors, serves to symbolize Stevens' need for intellectual stability in a world of constant change; green, on the other hand, a secondary color, a mixture of blue and yellow, perhaps comes closer to suggesting the "fluent mundo" that exists in the mind as well as externally.

A key poem in revealing Stevens' use of blue is "Landscape With Boat" (CP, 241–43). Here the poet assumes distance from his conflict by means of a persona, "an anti-master-man, floribund ascetic." Yet we should realize that the ascetic is Stevens, or rather he represents that aspect of Stevens' own nature which continually denies the senses. For Stevens, the error of the ascetic is not that he wishes to get beyond his physical limitations but that he is contemptuous of the world he shares, and consequently of himself as part of nature:

> He brushed away the thunder, then the clouds,
> Then the colossal illusion of heaven. Yet still
> The sky was blue. He wanted imperceptible air.
> He wanted to see. He wanted the eye to see
> And not be touched by blue. He wanted to know,
> A naked man who regarded himself in the glass
> Of air, who looked for the world beneath the blue,
> Without blue, without any turquoise tint or phase,
> Any azure under-side or after-color.

But what he finds at the "neutral center" or "the single-colored, colorless, primitive" is not *the* truth, the mystic's unity, beyond the limitations of both the physical scene and the mind's blue. It is a phantom, or a platonic "ghost," that drives him back to earth. Such illumination costs too dearly; to achieve it one must choose "not to live, to walk in the dark." The poem ends in a manner usual to Stevens. The poet has discovered his own fallacious thinking, which he has understood by projecting it through a persona. Consequently, he returns man to his limited, colorfully fragmented world and to his humanistic role:

He never supposed
That he might be truth, himself, or part of it,
That the things that he rejected might be part
And the irregular turquoise, part, the perceptible blue
Grown denser, part . . .

When the divinity of all "things" is accepted the truth is no longer a goal; it remains unexpressed, a "celestial pantomine," just as it is a "pantomine" in "Thirteen Ways of Looking at a Blackbird" (CP, 92–95). Its color and rhythm can, however, be *experienced,* for "if nothing was the truth, then all/ Things were the truth, the world itself was the truth." The perceptible blue is ultimately more desirable than the idea of blue.

Linked as it is with the mind, blue often can be the force that alienates man from the natural world, making him conscious of disembodied forms rather than "living form." In the Christian art of the Middle Ages, both blue and gold symbolized the ideal perfection which comes from heaven and contains no corrupting worldliness. Knowing as we do Stevens' love for the delightful imperfections of the world, we can understand why he never was completely happy with a color which emphasizes the divided nature of man: one half aspiring to ideal purity, the other enjoying things as they are. At times, Stevens conceives of blue as "this dividing and indifferent blue," and not as the Christian symbol of perfection or the ideal *azure* of Mallarmé.[32] Like the impressionist painters, Stevens alters the symbolic quality of blue:

From being the symbol of the alluring faraway world, it was transformed into the symbol of the remoteness of man from objects; it now tinged the entire image of nature for those who lived outwardly separated from what was near to their hearts and who preferred to concern themselves with the outward forms of things as they receded into the distance.[33]

The color blue can provide temporary relief from the dynamic conflicts of living, but it can also keep man from actual participation in "the freshness of the leaves, the burn/ Of the colors . . ." (CP, 231), which describes the "Bouquet of Belle Scavoir." Separated from the woman, the speaker of this poem is somewhat comforted by the memory of her "form" as it once existed in nature. But the thought is not satisfying:

> The sky is too blue, the earth too wide.
> The thought of her takes her away.
> The form of her in something else
> Is not enough.

As we saw with other poems (e.g., "Peter Quince at the Clavier") Stevens must incarnate beauty before he can realize it, realization being both understanding and fulfillment. Likewise colors cannot remain abstract forms — the blue guitar is a "form" (CP, 169) — but must find their existence in concrete particulars. Blue is like a sky or a sea that absorbs particulars, dilutes their individuality. Since the earth with its humanity is all that one can know, abstractions must be brought down to earth, as in "Woman Looking at a Vase of Flowers" (CP, 246–47):

> Hoot, little owl, within her, how
> High blue became particular
> In the leaf and bud and how the red,
> Flicked into pieces, points of air,
> Became — how the central, essential red
> Escaped its large abstraction, became,

202 Images of Wallace Stevens

First, summer, then a lesser time,
Then the sides of peaches, of dusky pears.

Hoot how the inhuman colors fell
Into place beside her . . .

Stevens' use of color further illustrates one of his central ideas: that the world is in motion, a state of continual fluency. But another Heraclitean belief shared by Stevens, and one less often commented on, is that, despite the flux of things, everything is unified and innately harmonious. Philip Wheelwright writes of Heraclitus:

It is misleading to call Heraclitus a pluralist without adding that he is somehow a monist as well, or to stress his doctrine of change, chance, and strife without adding that these characteristics, real and basic though they are, exist somehow counterbalanced by a tendency toward order, pattern, and harmony, which is equally inherent in what we must call (knowing that words fail us here) reality.[34]

The "hidden harmony" of Heraclitus is evident when he writes "Listening not to me but to the Logos, it is wise to acknowledge that all things are one." This concept is paralleled in Stevens by such apparently facetious statements as "the deer and the dachshund are one" (CP, 210), but nowhere is it more extensively revealed than in the poet's use of color. If blue is associated with the mind and green with the physical world, the world of sensations, then we would expect that Stevens would attempt to blend the two colors and make what he calls an "interpenetration of imagination and reality."

The poet's use of colors seems no more or less consist-

ent than his use of the ideas that the colors suggest. Both
the intellect and the imagination are blue, whereas the
life of sensation is green. A far more "reasonable" scheme
would have resulted from equating blue with reason,
green with sensation, letting the imagination act as neutral catalyst. Collingwood's definition, if not satisfactory, is at least clear: "Imagination is a distinct level of
experience intermediate between sensation and intellect, the point at which the life of thought makes contact
with the life of purely psychical experience." [35] As we
have seen, Stevens tries to distinguish the imagination
from reason—"It is the *mundo* of the imagination in
which the imaginative man delights and not the gaunt
world of the reason" (NA, 57–58)—but unfortunately
blue is the color of both, and "it is not always possible
to say that they are two" (NA, 150).

The urge to unify colors is quite overtly exhibited in
"A Primitive like an Orb" (CP, 440–43). In section III,
we are introduced to the familiar contrast:

> What milk there is in such captivity,
> What wheaten bread and oaten cake and kind,
> Green guests and table in the woods and songs
> At heart, within an instant's motion, within
> A space grown wide, the inevitable blue
> Of secluded thunder, an illusion, as it was,
> Oh as, always too heavy for the sense
> To seize, the obscurest as, the distant was . . .

Here clearly is seen the green "sensation function,"
spontaneous feeling "within an instant's motion." To be
the hedonist that he has been called would require that
Stevens accept this momentary delight as ultimate good.
He said himself that the poet's morality is the "morality

of the right sensation" (NA, 58), but Stevens' restless
mind will not ignore the "blue" that is "too heavy for the
sense/ To seize." He realizes that he exists both "within"
green and "within" blue, divisive as the thought may be.
In section VII, however, the colors are reconciled, inner
and outer worlds are "composed" in the poetic act—if
not in the act of living:

> The central poem is the poem of the whole,
> The poem of the composition of the whole,
> The composition of blue sea and of green,
> Of blue light and of green, as lesser poems,
> And the miraculous multiplex of lesser poems,
> Not merely into a whole, but a poem of
> The whole, the essential compact of the parts,
> The roundness that pulls tight the final ring . . .

No phrase could be more Heraclitean than "the essential compact of the parts," nor would we go wrong in
keeping it in mind when dealing with colors other than
blue and green. Looking at a checkered table cloth, for
example, the poet moves toward "a consciousness of
red and white as one" (CP, 450). Stevens persistently
attempts to "reconcile opposites" by simple coordinate
conjunctions if not by metaphor.[36]

In an early poem called "Architecture" (OP, 16–18),
which Stevens eliminated from the second edition of
Harmonium, we find the poet striving to construct a kind
of ivory tower, a "chastel de chasteté./ De pensée . . . ,"
with marble and pillars, in which he can ignore the
polarity of blue north and green south, by looking the
other way:

> Let us fix portals, east and west,
> Abhorring green-blue north and blue-green south.

We find Stevens, in a weak moment, attempting to retreat from the composite reality he advocated. The mingling of the blue north and the green south is clearly the integration of mind and body that the poet seeks, and yet it is offensive because, despite the poet's desires and protestations, the colors (as they embody concepts) can never be totally blended. The order achieved by the loss of individual "colors" would be unnatural and hence, for Stevens, unreal.

Caught in a dilemma of his own making, Stevens labors for an integration he despairs of. In "Idiom of the Hero" (CP, 200–01), he pictures the extraordinary man as one who realizes his fragmented nature and his own poverty and yet finds comfort in "things as they are."

> I heard two workers say, "This chaos
> Will soon be ended."
>
> This chaos will not be ended,
> The red and the blue house blended,
>
> Not ended, never and never ended,
> The weak man mended,
>
> The man that is poor at night
> Attended
>
> Like the man that is rich and right,
> The great men will not be blended . . .
>
> I am the poorest of all.
> I know that I cannot be mended,
>
> Out of the clouds, pomp of the air,
> By which at least I am befriended.

One can take red and blue as literal house colors or as
symbolic of the red of passion or the libido, which will
never be successfully dominated by the blue of the
rational mind. But to ignore the "value" of red and blue
is to fail to comprehend why the speaker "cannot be
mended"; in fact, to fail to see what is "broken" and in
need of restoration. The "blending" of blue and red
seems a figure for the "reconciliation of opposites" of
reason and passion, just as the blending of blue and
green stood for the interpenetration of imagination and
reality. The ending of "Idiom of the Hero" offers the
only consolation in a fallen world, a world of divided
colors which can never reenter the prism and return to
Dante's "heart of light." The hero is "befriended" by
his natural context, the "pomp of the air," just as the
player of the blue guitar, in the midst of his cerebral
melodies, declares: "Good air, my only friend" (CP, 175).

It is certainly doubtful that red is, as George McFadden says, "the color of the feebly real — red, the long,
low-frequency wave length of the light of the dying
stars. Red and its shades stand for the dying or dead
past." [37] There is little evidence to support removing
the image from its traditional associations with the intense glow of fire, with blood, and with the fructifying
power of the sun. Moreover, the color is almost exclusively active and energetic in all of its contexts, from
its earliest appearances as the red bird that flies across
the golden floor in "Le Monocle de Mon Oncle" (contrasting effectively with Yeats's "golden bird") and as
the "red of the sun" in the play *Three Travelers Watch
a Sunrise*. After blue and green, red is Stevens' favorite
color, appearing eighty-five times in the work. It is "red
weather" that Stevens finds as an image for the virile

imagination that counteracts the "Disillusionment of Ten O'Clock." [38]

Stevens almost never denies red an active role; it is frequently masculine or, more exactly, allied with the androgynous libido, and almost never diluted by reflection. Green, although certainly an image of "reality," sometimes can suggest a retreat from passionate activity, from engagement with disruptive human problems, an escape into Marvell's garden. Red, on the other hand, is the desire that refuses to be pacified by the "green shade." Associated with the sun, red is another expression of Blakean energy, potentially destructive as well as creative. This conflict between red and the cooler colors of blue and green is, like the conflict between sun and moon, a "war that never ends."

In "A Rabbit as King of the Ghosts" (CP, 209–10), for example, the rabbit's cat antagonist has a "red tongue" and a "green mind," the red suggesting the terrible actuality of the cat, its will and drive, which disturbs the serenity of the rabbit's world:

> There was the cat slopping its milk all day,
> Fat cat, red tongue, green mind, white milk
> And August the most peaceful month.

The poem records the progress of the rabbit's (and man's) rationalization by which he thinks away the red cat and is absorbed into the green grass where "there is nothing to think of." Once the libido has been suppressed, the rabbit is free to enjoy uninterrupted peace. The physical activity of the cat's "slopping" is balanced by the rabbit's passivity; it merely sits, serene as stone:

> The red cat hides away in the fur-light
> And there you are humped high, humped up,
>
> You are humped higher and higher, black as stone—
> You sit with your head like a carving in space
> And the little green cat is a bug in the grass.

The cat has been transformed from violent red into tranquil green, reduced in size and color by an "act of the mind" until it is tolerable.

Like the cat, the king of beasts in *Notes toward a Supreme Fiction* is awesome in his defiance of the "silence" or musical harmony with which Stevens frequently accompanies the color green.

> The lion roars at the enraging desert,
> Reddens the sand with his red-colored noise,
> Defies red emptiness to evolve his match,
>
> Master by foot and jaws and by the mane,
> Most supple challenger.   (CP, 384)

Both the cat and the lion act spontaneously and are therefore envied by the man, whose "violence" is never physically expressed. Poetry, as an "act of the mind" is blue, and often felt to be weak and ineffectual when juxtaposed with animal red. Although Stevens sees the need for dealing directly with the passions in poetry, he is, like his "ephebe" in *Notes toward a Supreme Fiction*, sometimes overpowered by their excess:

> You lie
> In silence upon your bed. You clutch the corner
> Of the pillow in your hand. You writhe and press
> A bitter utterance from your writhing, dumb,

> Yet voluble dumb violence. You look
> Across the roofs as sigil and as ward
> And in your centre mark them [the passionate
>   animals] and are cowed . . .   (CP, 384)

Another danger is that the passions may become too disciplined. One may "lash the lion" and his redness into submission, but consequently deprive poetry of its vital physical passions. Stevens' own verse is more often "blue" than "red," and he is aware of the limitations of his poetry. The poet, he realizes, must, like the ancient gods, be metamorphic:

> He is like a man
> In the body of a violent beast.
> Its muscles are his own . . .
>
> The lion sleeps in the sun.
> Its nose is on its paws.
> It can kill a man. (CP, 193)

Because blue is the color of the introspective mind, as the color fades further from the actual world and its vital green, it eventually diminishes until it becomes "the whiteness that is the ultimate intellect" (CP, 433). The color in the process is changed from a particular attribute into an abstraction, thereby allying it with the complex of images of mind previously discussed (north, cold, moonlight, etc.). The quietude produced by white, the purity of light before it is corrupted by man's kaleidoscopic world, is attractive to Stevens but, as usual, he is unable to pay the price it demands: separation from physical contact with change (his shifting blues and greens). Rather than an active opposing force, like Melville's white whale or the mysterious white that faces

Poe's A. Gordon Pym, Stevens' white is often the absence of color, that which is unnatural and cold.[39] Sometimes the color is associated with aging as prelude to death, as is the case with the "white elders" in "Peter Quince at the Clavier," and particularly with the pigeon in "Le Monocle de Mon Oncle":

> A blue pigeon it is, that circles the blue sky,
> On sidelong wing, around and round and round.
> A white pigeon it is, that flutters to the ground,
> Grown tired of flight.   (CP, 17)

The blue pigeon blends with its environmental blue; it is integrated with its surroundings, and not like man who experiences "this dividing and indifferent blue" or other conflicting colors. It follows the circular movement that Stevens finds in natural process. On the other hand, the white pigeon is a part of "the white of an aging afternoon" (CP, 412) that leads to eventual dissolution.

Besides its association with diminishing physical life, white at other times suggests the intellect when it cultivates abstraction and denies contact with *things* or with the imagination. Stevens, as we saw, turns the "white" animal in "The Apostrophe to Vincentine" into a creature "warm as flesh," wearing a "green" dress. This transformation aims, I believe, at incarnating beauty, bringing down to earth the "figured" nude who is anemic outside nature. The change from white to green simply illustrates the prime lesson of "Peter Quince at the Clavier":

> Beauty is momentary in the mind—
> A fitful tracing of a portal;
> But in the flesh it is immortal.

Stevens persistently courts a paradox: he yearns for the white of the "ultimate intellect" while acknowledging that such purity cannot be maintained in the actual world.[40] Like his snowman, he perceives the nothingness that white points toward and insists on confronting it. In "Credences of Summer" when he is near "The point of survey, green's green apogee," the poet still must imagine the abstraction that lies in the center:

> Trace the gold sun about the whitened sky
> Without evasion by a single metaphor.
> Look at it in its essential barrenness
> And say this, this is the centre that I seek.
> Fix it in an eternal foliage.   (CP, 373)

The center is meaningful only when it is, as it were, superimposed on the actual; it is the foliage that is "eternal." Although white may be at the center of all knowledge, it must be discovered only to be absorbed into "the floridest reality" (CP, 366). Like "nothingness," white is a separation from the living world of change, and Rudolf Arnheim's description of the color is close to what Stevens has in mind:

White is completeness and nothingness. Like the shape of a circle it serves as a symbol of integration without presenting to the eye the variety of vital forces that it integrates, and thus is as complete and empty as the circle. Not so the complementary colors. They show completeness as the balance of opposites. They exhibit the particular forces that constitute the whole. The stillness of achievement appears as an integration of antagonistic tendencies.[41]

The accuracy of the quotation in describing Stevens' use of white is shown particularly in "From the Packet

of Anacharsis" (CP, 365–66), in which Stevens' quest
for ultimate values is expressed in the "circle" or the
cold perfection of "marble," but finally is realized only
in the "completeness as the balance of opposites." [42]
The poem opens with a description of the scene:

> The farm was white.
> The buildings were of marble and stood in marble light.
> It was his clarity that made the vista bright.

The observer speculates on how a painter might "com-
pose/ The scene in his gray-rose with violet rocks."
Such pretty coloring is offensive, and Stevens (in the
person of "Bloom") outlines the manner in which a
"world of white" (CP, 193) can be transformed from cold
fixity to the "floridest reality":

> In the punctual centre of all circles white
> Stands truly. The circles nearest to it share
>
> Its color, but less as they recede, impinged
> By difference and then by definition
> As a tone defines itself and separates
>
> And the circles quicken and crystal colors come
> And flare and Bloom with his vast accumulation
> Stands and regards and repeats the primitive lines.

There may be a center of white but, "impinged by difference," men as well as things of the world find their
true identities by separating themselves from the dead
white until they "quicken" into fire. Life's definition,
despite any abstract center, remains undefined. Thus
we are returned once again to Stevens' conception of
life, which parallels his conception of art. We found that

the poet, for the most part, was unable to accept the statue image as a satisfactory embodiment of art. It is not surprising then to discover that white is the adjective most often applied to statues in *Owl's Clover,* signifying abstract as opposed to living form:

> The statue is white and high, white brillianter
> Than the color white and high beyond any height
> That rises in the air. (OP, 64)

Out of the weather of change, away from the tempering heat of the sun, cold white marble stands as Stevens' image of lifeless perfection:

> White slapped on white, majestic, marble heads,
> Severed and tumbled into seedless grass,
> Motionless, knowing neither dew nor frost. (OP, 49)

One of the most revealing uses of white occurs, in "The Poems of Our Climate" (CP, 193–94). Contemplating some pink and white carnations in a white bowl, the poet is drawn to the immaculate perfection of the objects which are themselves arranged like a work of art, a still life whose serenity composes the surrounding scene:

> The day itself
> Is simplified: a bowl of white,
> Cold, a cold porcelain, low and round,
> With nothing more than the carnations there.

Like the jar in Tennessee, the round bowl affects its context, and the observer envisions a world as perfectly ordered as a work of art, a world of "complete simplicity" in which all of one's desires would be satisfied, "fresh

in a world of white." At the same time, he realizes that
the only form or order he can experience in life or art
must somehow involve the flaws of man and nature.

> There would still remain the never-resting mind,
> So that one would want to escape, come back
> To what had been so long composed.
> The imperfect is our paradise.
> Note that, in this bitterness, delight,
> Since the imperfect is so hot in us,
> Lies in flawed words and stubborn sounds.

The human condition (that Keats called "a burning forehead and a parching tongue," and Stevens the imperfect
"so hot in us") is what the poet finally settles for. The
peace of a "white abstraction" (CP, 276) is never ultimately preferable to "an abstraction blooded" (CP, 385).

Black, the other non-color, has for Stevens the customary overtones of finality and death, the limitation
placed on man's knowledge. The color is the essential
shadow, the negation toward which all colors deepen
and which must be acknowledged before earth's colors
can be appreciated and affirmed. Like "nothingness" it
exists to be opposed, and like death it is the "mother of
beauty." The poet sometimes aspires to the ideal knowledge suggested by white, but he never forgets that in
the end white is a fiction that the fact of black mortality
contradicts.

"Thirteen Ways of Looking at a Blackbird" (CP, 92–
93) deals with the necessity of accepting human limitations. Life in the poem is a "pantomime" and the cause
or motive for all human action is "indecipherable."
Placed on a cold planet that is warmed from an outside
source, and where God is unknowable, the human ani-

mal must nevertheless relentlessly engage himself with physical reality and not retreat into illusions:

> O thin men of Haddam,
> Why do you imagine golden birds?
> Do you not see how the blackbird
> Walks around the feet
> Of the women about you?

Even the human imagination is weakened and ineffectual when it divorces itself from "seeing" what actually exists. The artificial golden bird of Yeats seems foreign beside Stevens' local *m*/*mento mori*. Equally deplorable is the man who isolates himself from physical contact "in a glass coach." His fear results from his inability to distinguish illusion from *the thing*. Both "ways" of looking at the bird are evasions of reality.

The poem's central theme, despite a fragmentary presentation, is the necessity of seeing the blackbird as a part of the world and, by extension, death as part of the universe.[43] Stevens finds unity in all life. Thus "A man and a woman and a blackbird/ Are one," and only the ignorant man would deny that the "blackbird is involved/ In what I know." Since knowledge is relative to the physical earth, and since the earth is forever in motion, a "fluent mundo," man's logic is built on shaky premises: "The river is moving./ The blackbird must be flying." The presence of mortality within the fluent mundo is painful because it interrupts euphoric harmonies:

> At the sight of blackbirds
> Flying in a green light,
> Even the bawds of euphony
> Would cry out sharply.

The poem concludes—stops would be a more exact word [44]—by reducing all time to the present, which can be experienced through sensation. The future is in the present ("It was evening all afternoon"), and the present is coordinated with the future ("It was snowing/ And it was going to snow"). Eliot found that "Only through time is time conquered," but Stevens finds that the only knowledge man can discover is immediate and factual:

> The blackbird sat
> In the cedar-limbs.

Black mortality is inextricably a part of life's evergreens; it sits "in" not "on" them. The blackbird is the *thing itself* that the poet always returns to after speculative excursions because the "ultimate value is reality." He must face the power of blackness (a blackness without the sinister qualities felt by Hawthorne or Melville) in order to discover his lively, colorful self and world.

We find that Stevens' refusal to escape from the "realization" of black sometimes leads him to question his own art, which can be an *ignis fatuus*, a product of the deceptive imagination. Black, including the use of "black men," suggests an elemental response to life that includes a fatalistic acceptance of death. Like the blackbird, the buzzard serves as death emblem in "The Jack-Rabbit" (CP, 50):

> The black man said,
> "Now, grandmother,
> Crochet me this buzzard
> On your winding-sheet,
> And do not forget his wry neck
> After the winter."

To crochet the blackbird on the fabric of life is not to disguise reality but to intensify it. The imagination should not substitute for reality—the black should remain black—although it can provide temporary relief from the pain of contemplating "the shrouding shadows" (CP, 100). The problem is again presented, but hardly explained, in "Explanation" (CP, 72–73):

> Ach, Mutter,
> This old, black dress,
> I have been embroidering
> French flowers on it.
>
> Not by way of romance
> Here is nothing of the ideal,
> Nein,
> Nein.
>
> It would have been different,
> Liebchen,
> If I had imagined myself,
> In an orange gown,
> Drifting through space,
> Like a figure on the church-wall.

As in "The Emperor of Ice-Cream" where the sheet "on which she embroidered fantails" is probably unsuccessful at disguising the woman's mortality, her "horny feet," so in this case the "embroidering" seems an evasion of black, even though the creator realizes the limitations of the artifice: the "escapes" of both the romantic and the platonic. A purely imaginative, "orange" [45] flight, however, seems superior because it brings color to life but does not deny reality. Stevens' belief in poetry as an "act of the mind," and as ephemeral creation, is again revealed.

To acknowledge black is one thing; to cultivate it as the "color" of life is another. Excessive meditation on death leads to morbidity. Like Hamlet, the woman in "Another Weeping Woman" (CP, 25) has experienced a death and suffers the despair and hopelessness of the bereaved. But the poet warns her:

> Poison grows in this dark.
> It is in the water of tears
> Its black blooms rise.

The human mind is powerful enough to reduce all colors to black, as in the case of "The Old Woman and the Statue" from *Owl's Clover*. The imagination is normally paralleled with color-making light, but when it is absent the mind tends to subdue all colors, convert the living to the dead:

>   the black of what she thought
>   Conflicting with the moving colors there
>   Changed them, at last, to its triumphant hue . . .
>   (OP, 44)

Both women suffer from poverty of the imagination; they are "tortured" or made "destitute" by a black they cannot balance with color.

A final poem may serve as an illustration of the antithesis of color and black that, in turn, is a part of the pervasive pattern of opposites discussed in previous chapters. "Domination of Black" (CP, 8–9) is a strikingly "imagistic" poem that for many readers probably evokes only an emotional response. Like many Stevens' poems it is labeled obscure because its images rely heavily on personal associations that may be felt but never comprehended intellectually. However, a look at the imagery in light of Stevens' use of the same images in other poems reveals another instance of the conflict between permanence and change, a conflict that Stevens was frequently to express in terms of color. Life is color, actively changing, delightfully uncertain; black, which absorbs and negates all color, suggests the permanence of death.

The color opposition that Stevens sets up on the poem is reinforced by images that he continually uses to represent natural process: fall leaves, wind, fire, twilight, the planets themselves — all significantly "turning" within the Heraclitean flux. The time of year is autumn, the season of change; the time of day is twilight, the hour of change; and the colorful tails of the peacocks are undeniably a part of the scene. Contrasting with these images of natural change are the "heavy hemlocks," which do not change with the seasons; their evergreen, approaching black, links them with the power of annihilation, the "striding night."

> I saw how the night came,
> Came striding like the color of the heavy hemlocks . . .

The tension between these two conflicting forces (the various colors of "bushes," "leaves," and peacocks' tails opposing the single color of black) makes the poem. Because the poem is the experience, the poet makes no comment. He offers no solution to the peacock's predicament, which is the human predicament: one opposes death but in seeking permanence does not one also oppose the self-destructive process of change which is life itself? Is the peacock's cry against the turning of all things or is it "against the hemlocks"? By identifying with the peacock, Stevens is able to objectify his dilemma without offering a resolution which at best would be only one man's resolution. Stevens' questioning response is remarkably like that of Keats in "Ode To a Nightingale," in which the poet, caught in a similar dilemma, wishing to identify with permanence yet bound to his own changing nature, can only question: "Do I wake or sleep?"

Stevens' "reality" is composed of the sun's colors, as well as the colors created by the interior sun of the imagination, and the black backdrop of death which they play against. After the poet "sees" the night and "hears" the peacocks, he has felt, if not understood, the human condition, his own mortality:

> I felt afraid.
> And I remembered the cry of the peacocks.

The peacock's cry is an affirmative act which resembles all human utterance, the colorful poem that both accepts and defies the "Domination of Black."

AFTERWORD

> "This man loved earth, not heaven,
> enough to die."
>
> *The Men That Are Falling*

The foregoing discussion, I believe, attests to the tenacity with which Stevens held to certain images that expressed his world-view. Although I have arbitrarily separated them into categories or opposing pairs, for ease of discussion, they exist as a totality. Each poem is an instance of a continual meeting of opposites: the fluctuation between sun and moon, the alternation between north and south, the vacillation between the guitar's blue and reality's green reveal a mind that changes, like the seasons, to no end

> Except the lavishing of itself in change,
> As light changes yellow into gold and gold
> To its opal elements . . . (CP, 416)

But it is also a mind whose vacillation occurs between poles that persistently recur; and therefore, in a profound way, there is little change at all.

Stevens' lack of any systematic philosophy or belief provides certain positive capabilities. Freed of the restrictions of what Keats called "consequitive reasoning" the poet is able to use the imagination to help make "Adam's dream" a reality. When Stevens at the opening of *Notes toward a Supreme Fiction* instructs his ephebe to "become an ignorant man again" and to see the sun "in the idea of it" (CP, 380), he is promoting what he calls in one of his very last poems "a new knowledge of reality" (CP, 534). It is a knowledge based on sensation, an awareness resulting from feeling.[1] To see the "idea" of the sun is to *feel* the life of the sun, without mental encumbrances. Stevens' escapes from sensory experience are as vital a part of his poetry as are any of his more celebrated epicurean traits, but his escapes into abstraction are cultivated only as a means of apprehending the full quality of the physical world. In Stevens, it is the human imagination, and not reason, that makes it possible for us to *conceive* of the world we live in; it is also the imagination that helps us *perceive* the harmonies of that world. Like Coleridge, Stevens believes that imagination is the soul of poetry, that it harmonizes or unifies diversity, and that it is analogous to the creative power of God. Also like Coleridge he believes that pleasure, not truth, is the end of poetry. But Stevens often goes further: one must clear the conceptual mind, deny the possibility of knowing the truth, before one can enjoy the satisfactions that are at hand.

On the Road Home

It was when I said,
"There is no such thing as the truth,"
That the grapes seemed fatter.
The fox ran out of his hole.

> You . . . You said,
> "There are many truths,
> But they are not parts of a truth."
> Then the tree, at night, began to change,
>
> Smoking through green and smoking blue,
> We were two figures in a wood.
> We said we stood alone.
>
> It was when I said,
> "Words are not forms of a single word.
> In the sum of the parts, there are only the parts.
> The world must be measured by eye";
>
> It was when you said,
> "The idols have seen lots of poverty,
> Snakes and gold and lice,
> But not the truth";
>
> It was at that time, that the silence was largest
> And longest, the night was roundest,
> The fragrance of the autumn warmest,
> Closest and strongest.   (CP, 203–04)

The physical world becomes more acutely real when we refuse to impose any meaning on it.

Since for Stevens sensation is the origin and end of knowledge, he is distrustful of images of permanence and attracted to images of ephemerality and change. In a late poem, "St. Armorer's Church from the Outside" (CP, 529–30), the poet is still employing images of south, sun, and color while playing a variation on the old opposition between statue and wilderness. Like Wordsworth's Tintern Abbey or Eliot's Little Gidding the church is in ruin, and Stevens characteristically looks from outside, from a natural viewpoint. The dead

permanence of the structure is for him analogous to the
fixed dogma of Christianity, a "truth" remote from the
rich, "geranium-colored day":

> St. Armorer's was once an immense success.
> It rose loftily and stood massively; and to lie
> In its church-yard, in the province of St. Armorer's,
> Fixed one for good in geranium-colored day.

The church was a haven for those who, unlike Stevens,
sought to be fixed for good. It *was* a great success, but
like the myth it symbolized, it was overcome by the
wilderness of natural change, of "reality":

> What is left has the foreign smell of plaster,
> The closed-in smell of hay. A sumac grows
> On the altar, growing toward the lights, inside.
> Reverberations leak and lack among holes . . .

The luxuriant green sumac suggests the wilderness, and
the altar man's artificial forms, his statues, even the
traditions by which he attempts to impose a meaningful
order on history as well as on external nature. Like the
jar in Tennessee, the altar is juxtaposed with sprawling
nature, but whereas in the earlier "Anecdote of the
Jar" a precarious balance is maintained, here the man-
made form (possibly because it suggests more of religious dogma than of imaginative artistic creation) is
defeated by "things as they are." Finally, Stevens
rejects the assurances of both religion and art, choosing
instead the uncertainties of an "always incipient cosmos"
(OP, 115), the unfixed "newness" and "freshness" of
the "geranium-colored day."
   A new "chapel" rises from the remains of the anti-

quated church, a human affirmation amid "Terre Ensevelie." But it is not a substantial, artificial creation, only an ephemeral "chapel of breath" which is *not* a symbol: "no sign of life but life,/ Itself . . ." Stevens' desire for living form caused him to find even Matisse's efforts to rejuvenate Christianity unsatisfying. Recalling the chapel at Vence, and probably the discussions about the relationship of contemporary art to religion, Stevens admires the painter's efforts, but seems more interested in the physical world of Provence (suggesting his own "sun" and "south") than he is in the admirable chapel that Matisse considered his finest and ultimate achievement.

> It is like a new account of everything old,
> Matisse at Vence and a great deal more than that,
> A new-colored sun, say, that will soon change forms
> And spread hallucinations on every leaf.

The rest of the poem declares "the need to be actual," to enjoy the "ruddy-ruby fruits" of life, the beauty of transience. Like Marius the Epicurean, Stevens seems to say, "How reassuring, after so long a debate about the rival *criteria* of truth, to fall back upon direct sensation, to limit one's aspiration after knowledge to that."

> St. Armorer's has nothing of this present,
> This *vif*, this dizzle-dazzle of being new
> And of becoming, for which the chapel spreads out
> Its arches in its vivid element,
>
> In the air of newness of that element,
> In an air of freshness, clearness, greenness, blueness,
> That which is always beginning because it is part
> Of that which is always beginning, over and over.

The "new" creation of Matisse, the artifact, is like all
of man's achievements finally subordinate to the colorful world from which it draws its sustenance. The poem
proposes a "chapel of breath" (man) and a "chapel
underneath St. Armorer's walls" (nature) but the chapel
itself (formal religion or art) is empty of everything but
"reverberations."

Although Stevens does not impose meaning on experience, he does by a subtle shifting of images provide the
materials from which the aroused reader can formulate
his own unity. His often perplexing juxtaposition of
images, the bizarre resemblances of a poem like "Sea
Surface Full of Clouds," is aimed at achieving for the
reader a sense of the "newness" the "freshness" of "that
which is always beginning, over and over." Two things
placed side by side create a third thing which is our
awareness of their relationship. Although Stevens never
achieves the integration of the opposites that he found
characterized his world, he does compel the reader to
reassess his own definition of "reality," to unmake his
made-up mind and discover the creative possibilities
that feeling affords. In many of Stevens' poems we are
jarred into a new way of looking at the familiar world.

Stevens' diction also frequently aims at jarring the
reader into a reevaluation of what exists and of the imagination, which can affect what exists. Through what
Henri Focillon calls a "dislocation of familiar verbal
molds" [2] the poet more often intensifies than clarifies
the subjects of his poems; through eccentric language
he creates a perspective that helps the reader apprehend
his own center, or whatever center there may be. "Life's
nonsense," the poet wrote in *Notes toward a Supreme
Fiction*, "pierces us with a strange relation" (CP, 383).

It is a relationship, rather than a meaning, that Stevens' language consistently provides. His preoccupation with curious and curious-sounding words is not evidence of obscurantism, but of the poet's desire to help the reader find pleasure in "things unintelligible, yet understood" (CP, 156). Language becomes an aspect of reality, and because "the physical world is meaningless tonight/ And there is no other" (CP, 337), the poet plays his guitar and enjoys being part of the mystery. The poems speculate on meaning and order, but, to use Herrick's words, they "delight in disorder," and like "reality" they sometimes remain happily obscure, an amalgam of sense and non-sense. Jung could have had Stevens in mind when he wrote:

Life is crazy and meaningful at once. And when we do not laugh over the one aspect and speculate about the other, life is exceedingly drab, and everything is reduced to the littlest scale. There is then little sense and little nonsense either. When you come to think about it, nothing has any meaning, for when there was nobody to think, there was nobody to interpret what happened. Interpretations are only for those who don't understand; it is only the things we don't understand that have any meaning. Man woke up in a world he did not understand, and that is why he tries to interpret it.[3]

R. P. Blackmur, one of the earliest critics to see the possibilities in Stevens' language, said much the same thing: "Half our sleeping knowledge is nonsense; and when put in a poem it wakes."[4]

Stevens was continually facing the dismal prospect of what the world would be like without the diversions or escapes offered by the imagination, and his method was to alternate ways of seeing: in one poem the world is a

"nothingness" that art can only disguise; in another, it
is a harmonious, changing, colorful process, art being
simply an extension of natural creation. Stevens accepts
both ways. Sometimes in the same poem the two viewpoints are combined: what the world is is what the poet
wants it to be. Yeats found late in life that his circus
animals had deserted him. Alone and empty, after a
fruitless search for ideals, the poet rejected "those
masterful images" that "grew in pure mind" and found
his comfort and courage in being able to acknowledge his
own fundamental identity, what Stevens might call his
"poverty." Yeats found his strongest and most convinc-
ing passion as a lyric poet when, like Baudelaire, his
heart was laid bare, when he was able to confront and
accept "a mound of refuse" containing all the discarded
masks that had hidden him from the world and from
himself.

In a relatively early poem, "The Man on the Dump"
(CP, 201–03), Stevens placed himself in a situation
remarkably like that of Yeats in "The Circus Animals'
Desertion." The "man" is the poet and "the dump" is
not only previous literary tradition but the poet's own
figurative language as well. The poem opens with a
fanciful metaphor: "The sun is a corbeil of flowers the
moon Blanche/ Places there, a bouquet." Immediately,
however, the poet admits the futility of evading through
language the actual fact of what is before him. He continues: "Ho-ho . . . The dump is full/ Of images. Days
pass like papers from a press." What follows is an inven-
tory of the contents of the dump that reveals lovely
things (bouquets) and disgusting things (a cat in a paper
bag) as well as "the janitor's poems of every day."
Stevens tries again to evade the "Chaos and barbarism

of reality" by creating pleasing analogies, similes that
divert the mind from the hard fact of mortality and the
ephemeral nature of creation. The day "puffs *as* Cornel-
ius Nepos reads"; it "puffs *like* this or that"; the green
"smacks *like* fresh water in a can, *like* the sea/ On a
cocoanut . . ." (My italics). The poet considers art as
Aristotelian imitations that have attempted to formalize
the transient things of the world, its "dew." ("How many
men have copied dew/ For buttons, how many women
have covered themselves/ With dew, dew dresses,
stones and chains of dew . . .") But all of these artifacts,
these images, because they are man-made, are finally
unsatisfying and "one grows to hate these things except
on the dump."

Only after rejecting the trash, after being purged of
artifice, is the poet able to *see* the reality he faces:

> Everything is shed; and the moon comes up as the moon
> (All its images are in the dump) and you see
> As a man (not like the image of a man),
> You see the moon rise in the empty sky.

Only after this realization of a world where "everything
is shed" does Stevens find his own independence from
any tradition, accepting the stoic comfort of being able
to strive, even when the sky is empty of gods and man
is without what Shaw called "the bribe of heaven."
Although Stevens' lines may not ring in the memory
with the power of Yeats's

> I must lie down where all the ladders start,
> In the foul rag-and-bone shop of the heart,

they nevertheless record a similar confrontation with reality and affirm a faith in the individual poet in isolation:

> One sits and beats an old tin can, lard pail.
> One beats and beats for that which one believes.
> That's what one wants to get near. Could it after all
> Be merely oneself, as superior as the ear
> To a crow's voice?

NOTES

Introduction

1. Quoted in Margaret Gilman, *The Idea of Poetry in France* (Cambridge, Mass.: Harvard University Press, 1958), pp. 200–01.

2. A. Alvarez, *The Shaping Spirit* (London: Chatto & Windus, 1958), p. 125.

3. G. S. Fraser, "The Aesthete and the Sensationalist," *Partisan Review*, XXII (Spring, 1955), 271.

4. *Kora in Hell: Improvisations* (Boston: Four Seas Co., 1920), pp. 17–18.

5. Paul Valéry, *The Art of Poetry*, trans. Denise Folliot (New York: Pantheon Books, 1958), p. 145.

6. *The Life of Forms in Art*, trans. C. Beecher Hogan and George Kubler (2nd ed.; New York: George Wittenborn, Inc., 1948), p. 36.

7. *Principles of Literary Criticism* (New York: Harcourt, Brace & Co., 1961), p. 119. Richards remarks: "Fifty different readers will experience not one common picture but fifty different pictures," p. 122.

8. Susanne K. Langer, *Problems of Art* (New York: Charles Scribner's Sons, 1957), p. 139.

9. John J. Enck, *Wallace Stevens: Images and Judgments* (Carbondale, Ill.: Southern Illinois University Press, 1964), pp. 108–09.

10. Quoted in Frank Kermode, *The Romantic Image* (New York: Chilmark Press, 1963), p. 138.

1 North and South

1. Friedrich Nietzsche, *The Birth of Tragedy and the Genealogy of Morals*, trans. Francis Colffing (New York: Doubleday & Co., Inc., Anchor Books, 1956), p. 28.

2. "Wallace Stevens: The World as Meditation," *The Achievement of Wallace Stevens*, ed. Ashley Brown and Robert S. Haller (Philadelphia: J. B. Lippincott Co., 1962), p. 217. Martz sees a "change" as instrumental in the evolution of Stevens' later meditative style, which he chiefly explores. There seems to be no evidence that Stevens changed subject matter; moreover, the poet explicitly stated his contempt for timely social problems in poetry (NA, 27). His themes or basic images shift but do not change.

3. "Wallace Stevens: The Life of the Imagination," *PMLA*, LXVI (1951), 567. Later, in *The Continuity of American Poetry* (Princeton: Princeton University Press, 1961), p. 382, Pearce added: "The late vision differs from the early in this: that at the end Stevens wants to conceive of confronting and knowing reality directly." I contend that an early poem such as "The Comedian as the Letter C" explores this

very problem, that Florida has not "proved sterile," and that the movement of Stevens' poetry has not been "away from the imagination's South." See John Finch, *Harvard Advocate* (Dec. 1940), p. 25.

4. I differ with Northrop Frye's interpretation of this image. He sees it as an act of mind that "destroys all form and particularity," in "The Realistic Oriole: A Study of Wallace Stevens," *Wallace Stevens: A Collection of Critical Essays*, ed. Marie Borroff (Englewood Cliffs, N.J.: Prentice-Hall, 1963), p. 163. I read "form gulping after formlessness" as natural form (the cyclical changes of the snake) opposed to chaos, the absence of form.

5. "Beyond Emerald and Amethyst," *Dartmouth College Library Bulletin*, IV (December, 1961), 61.

6. Quoted in Gilman, *The Idea of Poetry in France*, pp. 248–49.

7. C. G. Jung, *Symbols of Transformation*, trans. R. F. C. Hull (New York: Harper and Brothers, Harper Torchbooks, 1956), I, 178.

8. *Symbols of Transformation*, I, 218.

9. Kenneth Clark has investigated the long conflict between Venus Coelestis and Venus Naturalis. "Since the earliest times," he writes, "the obsessive, unreasonable nature of physical desire has sought relief in images, and to give these images a form by which Venus may cease to be vulgar and become celestial has been one of the recurring aims of European art." The ideal is never achieved, however, for "Botticelli's Venus 'born of the crystalline sea of thought and its eternity' has a piercing strain of sensuality; Rubens' Venus, a cornucopia of vegetable abundance, still aspires to the idea." See Kenneth Clark, *The Nude: A Study in Ideal Form* (New York: Pantheon Books, 1956), p. 71.

10. *Symbols of Transformation*, I, 99.

11. Trying to restore some of the dignity that the term "romantic" has lost, Stevens describes the contemporary romantic: "He happens to be one who still dwells in an ivory tower, but who insists that life would be intolerable except for the fact that one has, from the top, such an exceptional view of the public dump and the advertising signs of Snider's Catsup, Ivory Soap and Chevrolet Cars; he is the hermit who dwells alone with the sun and moon, but insists on taking a rotten newspaper" (OP, 256). Stevens is committed to actuality and change, but he is never *engagé*, as Malraux might use the term.

12. *Symbols of Transformation*, I, 178.

13. *The Comic Spirit of Wallace Stevens* (Durham, N.C.: Duke University Press, 1963), p. 9.

14. *Wallace Stevens*, p. 70.

15. *The Lost Son, and Other Poems* (New York: Doubleday & Co., Inc., 1948), p. 13.

16. Henri Bergson, *Creative Evolution,* trans. Arthur Mitchell (New York: The Macmillan Company, 1944), p. 312.

17. *The Art of Poetry,* p. 58.

18. Stevens' fascination with ephemeral creation is paralleled by Camus's in "Absurd Creation": "Art can never be so well served as by a negative thought. Its dark and humiliating proceedings are as necessary to the understanding of a great work as black is to white. To work and create 'for nothing,' to sculpture in clay, to know that one's creation has no future, to see one's work destroyed in a day while being aware that fundamentally this has no more importance than building for centuries — this is the difficult wisdom that absurd thought sanctions" (Albert Camus, *The Myth of Sisyphus* [New York: Alfred A. Knopf, Inc., 1955], p. 84).

19. Stephane Mallarmé, *Correspondance: 1862–1871,* ed. Henri Mondor (Paris: Gallimard, 1959), pp. 220–21.

20. *Creative Evolution,* p. 304.

21. Jean-Paul Sartre, *Being and Nothingness,* trans. Hazel E. Barnes (New York: Philosophical Library, 1956), p. 44.

22. *Wallace Stevens* (New York: Grove Press, Inc., 1961), p. 55.

23. *The Art of Poetry,* p. 180.

24. "Examples of Wallace Stevens," *The Achievement of Wallace Stevens,* p. 74.

25. For example: "Mud Master" (CP, 147); "God of the sausage-makers" (CP, 157); "Queen of Fact" (CP, 485); "The goober khan" (ruler of peanuts?) (CP, 142).

26. The following are further examples: "For realist, what is is what should be" (CP, 41); "It accepts whatever is as true,/ Including pain, which, otherwise, is false" (CP, 323); "Things stop in that direction and since they stop/ The direction stops and we accept what is/ As good" (CP, 374).

27. That Stevens looks favorably on the "muscular one" is supported by another poem in which the poet deplores the debilitating effect of the artificial and conventional:

> They ought to be muscular men,
> Naked and stamping the earth,
> Whipping the air.   (OP, 37)

28. *Mattino Domenicale ed altre poesie,* ed. and trans. Renato Poggioli (Torino: Giulio Einaudi, 1953), p. 182.

29. Edward E. Bostetter's remarks about the romantic poets are relevant to Stevens. He considers the romantic dependence upon elusive "imagination" as responsible for the uncertainty of purpose resulting in so many unfinished romantic poems: "The poet became

in reality the divine ventriloquist projecting his own voice as the voice of ultimate truth." See *The Romantic Ventriloquists* (Seattle: University of Washington Press, 1963), p. 7.

30. R. G. Collingwood, *The Principles of Art* (New York: Oxford University Press, 1958), p. 218.

31. *Birth of Tragedy*, p. 52.

32. Kermode, *Romantic Image*, p. 91.

33. Kermode defines Stevens' "poverty" as "the victory of reality over the imagination; or, the failure of the *fonction fabulatrice*" *(Wallace Stevens*, p. 65). This is misleading because although Stevens sometimes employs "poverty" in a negative way (CP, 10), he more often accepts it and transforms it into a positive value, the only redeeming knowledge man can find. Rather than representing a failure of the imagination, poverty contains a triumph since "the absence of the imagination had/ Itself to be imagined" (CP, 503). That Stevens both opposes *and* accepts poverty is made explicit in one of his *Adagia:* "Poetry is a purging of the world's poverty and change and evil and death. It is a present perfecting, a satisfaction in the irremediable poverty of life" (OP, 167).

34. *The Archetypes and the Collective Unconscious,* trans. R. F. C. Hull (New York: Pantheon Books, 1959), p. 15.

2 SUN AND MOON

1. *Symbols of Transformation*, II, 121.

2. "For both Plato and Kant the true reality lies above, behind, in short 'beyond' the phenomenon. Whether it was called 'idea' or *'das Ding an sich'* is relatively unimportant" (Thomas Mann, *Essays,* trans. H. T. Lowe-Porter [New York: Vantage Press, Inc., 1957], p. 263).

3. Stevens' realization of the limitations of human knowledge can be painful. In "From the Misery of Don Joost" (CP, 46), the speaker sees the sun as a part of the "storm" of reality he could never master:

> I have finished my combat with the sun;
> And my body, the old animal,
> Knows nothing more.

4. Stevens wants to believe that "reality is enough" and looks toward a state when he "sees without images." But, since a poet's words are often images, the poet ends up in a contradiction; he extols men whose "words have made a world that transcends the world and a life livable in that transcendence" (NA, 129–30).

5. Roy Harvey Pearce appears incorrect in saying that "generally in the poems 'sun' = 'reality,' and 'autumn'–like 'spring'– = the

poet's season, since it is one in which he is protected from the sun, yet is not, as in winter, denied it" (*The Continuity of American Poetry*, p. 379). Although Stevens sees "a war between the mind and sky," he does not hide: "the poet is always in the sun . . ." (CP, 407). Moreover, "autumn" appears less often than the other seasons: summer (124), spring (61), winter (61), autumn (49). (This count is taken from the *Concordance to the Poetry of Wallace Stevens*, ed. Thomas F. Walsh [University Park, Penn.: Pennsylvania State Univeristy Press, 1963].)

6. *Symbols of Transformation*, I, 89.

7. *The Poems of John Donne*, ed. Herbert Grierson (Oxford: The Clarendon Press, 1912), p. 135.

8. Jung comments that "the early Church stood in a special relationship to Christ as the *Sol novus*, and on the other hand had some difficulty in shaking off the pagan symbol" (*Symbols of Transformation*, I, 106). He further speculates that the nimbus around the head of Christ and the haloes of saints are traces of sun-worship preserved in religious art. Jacquetta Hawkes says that in Rome "when in the 1950's excavations were made below the cathedral in the hope of finding the tomb of St. Peter, this necropolis was found and in it the earliest known Christian mosaic. It showed Christ as sun driving a chariot with a flying cloak and a rayed nimbus behind his head" (*Man and the Sun* [New York: Random House, Inc., 1962], pp. 202–03).

9. *Symbols of Transformation*, I, 87. Jung asserts that while "one man will derive the idea of God from the sun, another will maintain that it is the numinous feelings it arouses which give the sun its godlike significance." He admits the impossibility of proof, but he believes that "psychic energy or libido creates the God-image by making use of archetypal patterns, and that man in consequence worships the psychic force active within him as something divine," p. 86. Stevens, however, is less committed: "It could be that the sun shines/ Because I desire it to shine or else/ That I desire it to shine because it shines" ("Desire & the Object" [OP, 85]).

10. Differing from Freud, Jung believes that this interior power, the libido, is "not the sexual instinct, but a kind of neutral energy, which is responsible for the formation of such symbols as light, fire, sun, and the like" (*Symbols of Transformation*, I, 139).

11. If God exists for Stevens he exists in the body of the world: "the poets who most urgently search the world for the sanctions of life . . . may find their solutions in a duck in a pond or in the wind on a winter night" ("The Irrational Element in Poetry" [OP, 222]).

12. Stevens clearly wished that human creativity could match

natural creativity: "If in the minds of men creativeness was the same thing as creation in the natural world, if a spiritual planet matched the sun . . ." ("Two or Three Ideas" [OP, 210]).

13. Susanne Langer indicates that artistic symbols, unlike symbols used in discursive reasoning, can be ambivalent: "I believe the power of artistic forms to be emotionally ambivalent springs from the fact that emotional opposites . . . are often very similar in their dynamic structure, and reminiscent of each other" (*Feeling and Form* [New York: Charles Scribner's Sons, 1953], p. 242).

14. Stevens (through Crispin) saw his age as "grovelling" on the "foot-ways of the moon" (CP, 28), addicted to illusion and unable to articulate man's condition in art. The poet believed that romanticism at its worst "is to poetry what the decorative is to painting" (*Adagia* [OP, 169]).

15. The creative imagination is, of course, androgynous, which perhaps explains the mingling of sun and moon in the invocation to the anima (or "White Goddess") at the beginning of "Le Monocle de Mon Oncle":

> "Mother of heaven, regina of the clouds,
> O sceptre of the sun, crown of the moon . . . (CP, 13)

16. At one stage, as Hillis Miller points out, Yeats saw sun and moon as symbols of God and the self, with man caught in a "rhythmic fluctuation" or "endless alternation" between the two. In general, Stevens supports Yeats's idea that there is a "conflict between Moon and Sun, or . . . between a Moon that has taken the Sun's light into itself, 'I am yourself,' and the Moon lost in the Sun's light, between Sun in Moon and Moon in Sun" (J. Hillis Miller, *Poets of Reality* [Cambridge, Mass.: Harvard University Press, 1965], p. 118).

17. There are 217 direct references to sun, 102 to the moon. In every volume, moreover, "sun" outnumbers "moon." There are twice as many references to "sun" in *Ideas of Order* and *Parts of a World*. The final *The Rock* contains seven times as many references to "sun."

18. Quoted in Guy Michaud, *Mallarmé*, trans. Marie Collins and Bertha Humez (New York: New York University Press, 1966), p. 139. A. G. Lehmann extends the quotation, making it central to his definition of "symbolism": "Nommer un objet, c'est supprimer les troi quarts de la jouissance de poème qui est faite du bonheur de deviner peu à peu; le suggerer, voilà le rêve. C'est le parfait usage de ce mystère qui constitue le symbol: evoquer petit à petit un objet pour montrer un état d'ame" (*The Symbolist Aesthetic in France* [Oxford: Basil Blackwell & Mott, Ltd., 1950], p. 299).

19. Stevens' corrective for the woman's condition occurs in "The Well Dressed Man with a Beard": "After the final no there comes a yes/ And on that yes the future world depends./ No was the night. Yes is this present sun" (CP, 247).

20. "The sun comparison tells us over and over again," says Jung, "that the dynamic of the gods is psychic energy. This is our immortality, the link through which man feels inextinguishably one with the continuity of all life" (*Symbols of Transformation*, I, 202). Stevens supports this idea: "To know that the change and that the ox-like struggle/ Come from the strength that is the strength of the sun,/ Whether it comes directly or from the sun" (CP, 205).

21. "Wallace Stevens and The Symbolist Imagination," *The Act of the Mind* (Baltimore: The Johns Hopkins Press, 1965), p. 99.

22. "Wallace Stevens," p. 100.

23. Here Stevens' use of "golden" illustrates the general problem of making his image patterns rigidly fixed. Gold is frequently linked with the sun or male principle, e.g., "The sun is gold, the moon is silver" (OP, 29). Is the poet subconsciously desirous of making the myth active and vital once more, of giving himself to the "illusion"?

24. *The Philosophy of Literary Form* (New York: Alfred A. Knopf, Inc., Vintage Books, 1957), p. 21.

25. *Endymion*, I, 608–10.

26. As Jung says, "The first carrier of the anima-image is the mother" and "the feminine belongs to man as his own unconscious femininity, which I have called the anima" (*Symbols of Transformation*, II, 283:437).

27. William Butler Yeats, *Essays and Introductions* (London: Macmillan & Co., Ltd., 1961), p. 94.

28. R. G. Collingwood, *The Principles of Art* (New York: Oxford University Press, 1958), p. 336.

29. Stevens' attitude toward the moon here and in numerous poems reinforces the view that in "Farewell to Florida" the poet is not finally rejecting the sensational south in favor of the cerebral north. Although "the moon/ Is at the masthead and the past is dead," and "high above the mast the moon/ Rides clear of her mind . . . ," the poem is made more meaningful in the light of Stevens' other uses of moon. The poet would never permanently commit himself to a symbol that can suggest illusion, isolation, and often sterile introspection.

30. *The Enchaffed Flood*, or *The Romantic Iconography of the Sea* (New York: Random House, Inc., 1950), p. 7.

31. *The Comic Spirit of Wallace Stevens* (Durham, N.C.: Duke University Press, 1963), pp. 103–05. Frank Kermode, who admires

the poem, would support a more affirmative reading. He believes that it is a "handling of another theme in *Notes*, the animal consciousness imposing its order on reality, as opposed (here tacitly) to the human, which discovers an order without imposing it" (*Wallace Stevens*, p. 76).

32. *A Vision* (New York: The Macmillan Company, 1956), p. 136.

33. Stevens here would agree with Kierkegaard that "genius is not teleologically situated in regard to the world and to others." His mixture of pride and humility often reminds one of Kierkegaard's statement: "It is modest of the nightingale not to require anyone to listen to it; but it is also proud of the nightingale not to care whether any one listens to it or not" (*The Living Thoughts of Kierkegaard*, ed. W. H. Auden [New York: David McKay Company, 1952], pp. 100–01).

34. Two quotations from Stevens' essays illustrate the poet's association of the imagination and light:

I think that his function is to make his imagination theirs [his readers] and that he fulfills himself only as he sees his imagination become the light in the minds of others (NA, 29).

Like light, it [the imagination] adds nothing, except itself. What light requires a day to do, and by day I mean a kind of Biblical revolution of time, the imagination does in the twinkling of an eye (NA, 61–62).

35. George D. Painter, *Proust: The Early Years* (Boston: Little, Brown & Co., 1959), p. 313.

36. Stevens' use of candle, lantern, lamp, etc., as images of the imagination accords with the romantic iconography described by Meyer Abrams in *The Mirror and The Lamp* (New York: Oxford University Press, 1953). Stevens' "romanticism" is affirmed by his frequent choice of the egoistic image:

> The quiet lamp
> For this creator is a lamp
> Enlarging like a nocturnal ray
> The space in which it stands . . .   (OP, 100).

37. Stevens never maintains for long a static situation in which man's light dominates reality. As the candle is dominated by the wind, so are the chandeliers in "The Blue Buildings in the Summer Air" dominated by external forces: "The shore, the sea, the sun,/ Their brilliance through the lattices, crippled/ The chandeliers . . ." (CP, 217). The mastering power of reality may also help explain the difficult line "The moonlight/ Fubbed the girandoles" (CP, 11).

38. "No longer do I believe," wrote Stevens, "that there is a mystic muse . . . I am myself a part of what is real, and it is my own speech and the strength of it, this only, that I hear or ever shall" (NA, 60).

3 MUSIC AND THE SEA

1. *The Art of Poetry*, p. 42. Mallarmé wrote to René Ghil that the duty of poetry was "to take everything back from music." See Michaud, *Mallarmé*, p. 113.

2. Stevens uses the figure of the rabbi in several poems (CP, 17, 134, 389). He chose the figure, he said, because he is a "man devoted in the extremes to scholarship and at the same time to making some use of it for human purposes" (*Mattino Domenicale ed altre poesie*, ed. and trans. Renato Poggioli [Turino: Giulio Einaudi, 1953], p. 185).

3. Similar lines, imaging speech as a "twanging instrument," occur in *Owl's Clover* (OP, 63):

> It may be the future depends on an orator,
> Some pebble-chewer practiced in Tyrian speech,
> An apparition, twanging instruments
> Within us hitherto unknown . . .

4. *Mattino Domenicale*, p. 179.

5. Stevens refers to himself as Ariel in "The Planet on the Table" (CP, 532).

6. The sea is the Jungian image for the unconscious, as well as an image for natural fecund power. It is that unknown depth which must be brought to consciousness by the poet. It is, as Frank Kermode says, Stevens' "basic, inarticulate reality" (*Wallace Stevens*, p. 70).

7. *The Life of Forms in Art*, quoted in NA, 46.

8. As Collingwood says, "The work of art proper is something not seen or heard, but something imagined . . ." and "The music to which we listen is not the heard sound, but that sound as amended in various ways by the listener's imagination . . ." (*The Principles of Art*, pp. 142, 143).

9. "Music is not the cause or the cure of feelings, but their *logical expression*" (Susanne K. Langer, *Philosophy in a New Key* [New York: Mentor Books, 1948], p. 185).

10. The similarity of Stevens and Valéry is revealed in their poetic method. Valéry wrote: "I should be tempted (if I followed my inclinations) to engage poets to produce, like musicians, a diversity of variants or solutions of the same subject. Nothing would seem to me more consistent with the idea I like to hold of a poet and of poetry" (*The Art of Poetry*, p. 145).

11. *Mattino Domenicale*, p. 179.

12. The music of the guitar provides another instance of Stevens' belief in "ephemeral creation." The sounds of the blue guitar are "like a buzzing of flies in autumn air" (CP, 166). Artistic form resembles natural form: Its essence is change.

13. Stevens searches for a "true belief" but he admits that "the imagination (poor pale guitar) is not that. But the air, the mere *joie de vivre*, may be" (*Mattino Domenicale*, p. 179).

14. Stevens based the word on "oxide." He wished to suggest the far from idyllic industrial countryside many face every day as "reality" (*Mattino Domenicale*, p. 183).

15. Stevens' refusal to be committed either to fiction or to fact is seen as intellectual weakness by some critics. Wylie Sypher, for example, accuses Stevens of "evading the absolute, the total fiction" ("Connoisseur of Chaos," *Partisan Review*, XIII [1946], 87). Others, more sympathetic to the poetry itself, still find that "if we follow the dialectic to which such imagination is committed, we will find ourselves trapped in the *cul-de-sac* of an aesthetic and moral relativism" (Newton P. Stallknecht, "Absence in Reality: A Study in the Epistemology of the Blue Guitar," *Kenyon Review*, XXI [1959], 557). Stevens wants, however, what he calls "thinkers without final thoughts/ In an always incipient cosmos . . ." (OP, 115). Hence he refuses to resolve the dilemma he continually poses.

16. *The Heritage of Symbolism* (New York: St. Martin's Press, Inc., 1961), p. 2.

17. "The essential fault of surrealism," Stevens writes, "is that it invents without discovering. To make a clam play an accordion is to invent not to discover. The observation of the unconscious, so far as it can be observed, should reveal things of which we have previously been unconscious . . ." (*Adagia* [OP, 177]). Crispin, like the singer in this poem, reveals himself.

18. Auden, *The Enchafèd Flood*, p. 7. Although this work does not deal with Stevens directly, it deals with the sea image as it is employed by romantic and symbolist writers.

19. *Coleridge on Imagination* (Bloomington, Indiana: Indiana University Press, 1960), p. 57.

20. "The poet seems to confer his identity on the reader," wrote Stevens. "It is easiest to recognize this when listening to music — I mean this sort of thing: the transference" (*Adagia* [OP, 158]).

21. Stevens' desire for the new sometimes approaches perversity:

> Perhaps if the orchestras stood on their heads
> And dancers danced ballets on top of their beds —
> We haven't tried that. (OP, 42)

22. See also NA, 179.

23. *Philosophy in a New Key*, p. 197. Mrs. Langer cites music as highly symbolic; in fact, it can "articulate forms which language cannot set forth."

24. Stevens characteristically avoids definition. Like "nobility," the one of fictive music "resolved itself into an enormous number of vibrations, movements, changes. To fix it is to put an end to it" (NA, 34).

25. Quoted in Michaud's *Mallarmé*, p. 15.

26. *Philosophy in a New Key*, p. 199.

27. Quoted in C. K. Ogden and I. A. Richards, *The Meaning of Meaning* (New York: Harcourt Brace & Company, 1923), p. 43.

28. P. 291.

4 THE STATUE AND THE WILDERNESS

1. For example, as perceptive a critic as Howard Nemerov (*Poetry and Fiction* [New Brunswick, N.J.: Rutgers University Press, 1963], p. 83) writes of the statue as a favorable symbol for creative art (which it sometimes is); whereas in the majority of cases the image, as I hope to show, is an unfavorable one.

2. Allen Tate's criticism that "To Autumn" is a "very nearly perfect piece of style but it has little to say" could be applied to many of Stevens' poems which likewise celebrate man's image *in* external nature. Allen Tate, *On the Limits of Poetry: Selected Essays 1928–1948* (New York: William Morrow & Co., 1948), p. 168.

3. *Life of Forms in Art*, p. 35.

4. *Life of Forms in Art*, p. 6.

5. *The Art of Poetry*, p. 177.

6. *The Art of Poetry*, p. 140. Valéry stopped "Le Cimetière Marin" arbitrarily on a friend's advice, admitting that the poem had not ended, that he could create additional stanzas. See Valéry's introduction to Gustave Cohen's *Essai d'explication du cimetière marin* (Paris: Gallimard, 1958), p. 16: "c'est ainsi que *par accident* fut fixée la figure de cet ouvrage. Il n'y a point de mon fait." Stevens easily cut stanzas of "Sunday Morning" and neither version is noted for its logical progression.

7. Burnshaw comments on the controversy in *Sewanee Review*, LXIX (1961), 355–66.

8. *Mallarmé: Selected Prose Poems, Essays, and Letters*, trans. Bradford Cook (Baltimore: The Johns Hopkins Press, 1956), p. 13.

9. *The Art of Poetry*, pp. 70–71.

10. *Romantic Image*, p. 55.

11. *Romantic Image*, p. 86.

12. Nietzsche (*The Birth of Tragedy*, pp. 23–24) envisions the Dionysiac ritual: "Now that the gospel of universal harmony is sounded, each individual becomes not only reconciled to his fellow but actually at one with him. . . . He feels himself to be godlike and strides with the same elation and ecstasy as the gods he has seen in

his dreams. No longer the *artist,* he has himself become a *work of art:* the productive power of the whole universe is now manifest in his transport, to the glorious satisfaction of the primordial One."

13. Stevens, however, does not bring to his "wilderness" any of the sinister and mysterious qualities that Conrad does, say, in *Heart of Darkness.* Their absence may be felt to weaken the work dramatically or emotionally.

14. *Life of Forms in Art,* p. 35.

15. In "Thirteen Ways of Looking at a Blackbird" (CP, 92–95) Stevens expresses his acceptance of living over ideal form:

> O thin men of Haddam,
> Why do you imagine golden birds?
> Do you not see how the blackbird
> Walks around the feet
> Of the women about you?

16. *Life of Forms in Art,* p. 47.

17. *Selected Poems and Letters of John Keats* (Boston: Houghton Mifflin Company, 1959), p. 350.

18. T. S. Eliot, *The Complete Poems and Plays,* ed. N. Braybrooke (New York: Farrar, Straus & Cudahy, Inc., 1958), p. 125.

19. *Creative Intuition in Art and Poetry* (New York: Meridian Books, 1956), p. 50: "Art continues in its own way the labor of divine creation. It is therefore true to say with Dante that our human art is, as it were, the grandchild of God." Maritain links Stevens with Rimbaud, Mallarmé, Hart Crane, and other artists who deplore the historical sense and attempt to create new myths. "It is through history that the union of Nature and man is accomplished," writes Maritain (p. 7). In contrast to Stevens' definition of poetry as the "supreme fiction" Maritain offers: "Metaphysical myths are needed by poetry, but they cannot be provided by poetry" (p. 318).

Stevens advocates a life of irrationality and sensation for the poet in his essay "The Figure of the Youth as Virile Poet." He writes: "For all the reasons stated by William James, and for many more, and in spite of M. Jacques Maritain, we do not want to be metaphysicians" (NA, 59).

20. Stevens' method is explored in Sister M. Bernetta Quinn's *The Metamorphic Tradition in Modern Poetry* (New Brunswick, N.J.: Rutgers University Press, 1955), pp. 49–88.

21. *Marius the Epicurean* (New York: Modern Library, 1921), p. 106.

22. *Marius the Epicurean,* p. 122. The anti-Platonism of both Pater and Stevens, their essential kinship, is revealed in one way by

their use of the image of fire, which in turn allies them with the pre-Socratic Heraclitus.

23. *La Pesanteur et La Grâce* (Paris: Plon, 1948), p. 119. Stevens refers to this work in "The Relation Between Poetry and Painting" (NA, 174).

24. In "Negation," Stevens again reveals his rejection of an ideal: "Hi! The creator too is blind,/ Struggling toward his harmonious whole . . ." (CP, 97).

25. See "Easter 1916," *Collected Poems* (New York: The Macmillan Company, 1956), p. 177.

26. *The Myth of Sisyphus.* Stevens bears a striking resemblance to Camus. Both are often seen as hedonists; both find the world unknowable, yet constantly seek clarity and coherence in it; both are "convinced of the wholly human origin of all that is human" (p. 91). Both writers' fondness for the stone image is perhaps a clue to further affinity. See Camus' early short story "The Gift."

27. Ralph J. Mills, Jr., "Wallace Stevens: The Image of the Rock," *Accent*, XVIII (Spring, 1958), 75–89. Mills finds Stevens ambivalent: Though Stevens is "certainly aligned with Nietzsche, he is nevertheless unwilling to discard wholly the idea of God" (p. 78).

28. Alfred North Whitehead, *Science and the Modern World* (New York: The Macmillan Company, 1929), pp. 120–22.

5 COLORS AND "DOMINATION OF BLACK"

1. In a dark mood one could agree with A. G. Lehmann that because of the plethora of definitions of "symbolism" we should "expel the word from our histories of literature and our literary discussions, and try to find another to take its place" (*Symbolist Aesthetic in France*, p. 315). Hillis Miller writes of Stevens: "His images entirely contain their own reality. They are not symbolic. They are what they are" (*Poets of Reality*, p. 228). The semantic problem, however, is *what are they?* Colors do include meanings outside themselves. As Stevens wrote: "It is possible that to seem — it is to be,/ As the sun is something seeming and it is" (CP, 339). Again, Susanne Langer's distinction is as valuable as any: the art symbol "cannot strictly be said to have a meaning; what it does have is import" (*Problems of Art*, p. 139).

2. *Middle English Literature* (London: Methuen & Co., Ltd., 1951), p. 240.

3. André Malraux, *The Voices of Silence*, trans. Stuart Gilbert (New York: Doubleday & Co., Inc., 1953), p. 346.

4. Tindall writes: "His recurrent blue and green, north and south, moon and sun are signs for imagination and fact, not symbols"

(*Wallace Stevens* [Minneapolis, Minn.: University of Minnesota Press, 1961], p. 18).

5. *Wallace Stevens* (New Brunswick, N.J.: Rutgers University Press, 1958), p. 46.

6. *The Colour-Sense in Literature* (London: Ulysses Bookshop, 1931), p. 29. Ellis's very brief study is based on inconclusive data: He limits himself to only certain works of each poet investigated. Nevertheless, he is instructive in detecting "romantic" characteristics, ones which Stevens shares.

7. *Literature, Philosophy and the Imagination* (Bloomington, Ind.: Indiana University Press, 1962), p. 159.

8. Stevens' images are often symbolic, but they never constitute an allegory. "Symbols are not allegories and not signs," as Jung says. "They are images of contents which for the most part transcend consciousness" (*Symbols of Transformation*, I, 77).

9. "To study the so-called colour-symbolism of the Middle Ages is to see into a world where, even among adult and educated Europeans, the sterilizing of colour-sensa had not taken place: where any one who is conscious of seeing a colour is simultaneously conscious of feeling a corresponding emotion, as is still the case among ourselves with children and artists" (Collingwood, *The Principles of Art*, p. 162).

10. Stevens' colors are truly another language, for "just as the words of a language are a set of verbal conventions, so the imagery of poetry is a set of symbolic conventions. This set of symbolic conventions differs from a symbolic system, such as a religion or a metaphysic, in being concerned, not with content, but with a mode of apprehension" (Northrop Frye, *Fables of Identity* [New York: Harcourt Brace and World, Inc., 1963], p. 218).

11. *The Meaning of Meaning*, p. 176.

12. Both colors are affirmative, frequently associated with masculine strength or creative power. The sun is described as red many times, e.g., CP, 217, 243; OP, 143. " 'Why are you red/ In this milky blue?'/ I said./ 'Why sun-colored . . .' " (CP, 58). Gold is also associated with the sun: "The sun is gold, the moon is silver" (OP, 29). Further instances: CP, 133, 159, 373.

13. *Creative Intuition*, p. 50.

14. More precisely, "we imagine non-existent combinations of existing elements" (Ludwig Wittgenstein, *The Blue and Brown Books* [Oxford: Basil Blackwell & Mott, Ltd., 1958], p. 31). Rimbaud's famous color sonnet "Voyelles" employs concrete similes to convey what each vowel suggests, but the poem seems more surrealistic trick than imaginative act. He insists on his own creative power

over that of nature: "J'inventai la couleur des voyelles!" and "je me flattai d'inventer un verbe . . ." (Arthur Rimbaud *Oeuvres Complètes* [Paris: Gallimard, 1954], p. 233). For Stevens, "the essential fault of surrealism is that it invents without discovering" (OP, 177). And Valéry said much the same thing: "I can be interested only in things I cannot invent" (*The Art of Poetry*, p. 105).

15. Stevens opposes what he calls "a white abstraction" (CP, 385) and prefers instead "an abstraction blooded" (CP, 385). He would "choke every ghost with acted violence . . ." (CP, 155).

16. In an early poem "Mandolin and Liqueurs" (OP, 28) the same dissatisfaction with conformity occurs:

> If awnings were celeste and gay,
> Iris and orange, crimson and green,
> Blue and vermilion, purple and white,
> And not this tinsmith's galaxy,
> Things would be different.

Stevens' fanciful use of color, like his nonsense words, reminds one of Edward Lear. Besides the famous "pea-green" boat of "The Owl and the Pussycat," there are the "jumblies whose heads are green and whose hands are blue," birds whose wings are blue, and a King and Queen, "one in red, and one in green."

17. Coleridge's *The Rime of the Ancient Mariner* and Rimbaud's *Le Bateau Ivre* record introspective voyages much like that of Stevens' "The Comedian as the Letter C." All of these poems have a bare literal level, employing extensive color symbolism to achieve effects that conventional rhetoric cannot approach.

18. Kurt Badt, *Cézanne* (Berkeley: University of California Press, 1965), p. 59. Badt traces the history of the color blue in painting.

19. *Colour-Sense*, pp. 24–25.

20. *Colour-Sense*, p. 18.

21. Four critics of Stevens may be cited to indicate the general agreement on the image. Green is "the strictest reality" – Robert Pack; "the color of reality" – Frank Kermode; "used to suggest *livingness* and our involvement in the physical world" – William Van O'Connor; "color of vital force and change" – George McFadden. Stevens himself probably best defined it when he said, "my green, my fluent mundo" (CP, 407).

22. Marvell's fascination with green as an image of natural harmony, divorced from "the busy company of men," is well known. Like Stevens, he uses the color to suggest a tranquil mind, e.g., "a green thought in a green shade" and "companions of my thoughts more green. . . ." A line from "The Mower" is pure Stevens: "His

green seraglio has its eunuchs too." But Stevens is less consistent than Marvell. Green sometimes corresponds to "the violent pressure of reality, working from the external world upon the human spirit" (George McFadden, "Probings for an Integration: Color Symbolism in Wallace Stevens," *Modern Philology*, LVIII [Feb., 1961], 190).

23. Stevens discusses the myth of Narcissus in "Three Academic Pieces" (NA, 79–80).

24. Characteristically, Stevens contradicts himself. In another poem, "Things of August" (CP, 492), it is not the observer who changes reality; like a *tabula rasa,* he is the recipient of nature's acts:

> The world images for the beholder.
> He is born the blank mechanic of the mountains,
>
> The blank frere of fields, their matin laborer.
> He is possessed of sense not the possessor.
>
> He does not change the sea from crumpled tinfoil
> To chromatic crawler. But it is changed.

25. *Heraclitus* (New York: Atheneum Publishers, 1964), p. 15.

26. *The Art of Poetry*, p. 192.

27. Frank Kermode refuses to attribute Eliot's "dissociation" to the seventeenth century or to any specific period. "It is not merely a matter of wrong dates; however far back one goes one seems to find symptoms of dissociation." For Kermode, the concept seems more mythological than historical, and he finds "an implicit parallel with the Fall" (*Romantic Image*, p. 141).

28. A difference between Stevens and Frost suggests itself. In Frost's "The Most of It," the poet also seeks self-fulfillment, "counter-love, original response." But Frost's need is for something human, and his desire is frustrated by the arrival of the "great buck" out of the wilderness. Stevens' need is imaginative and egocentric, the "queen" approximating his "interior paramour." As he says in one of his *Adagia:* "Life is an affair of people not of places. But for me life is an affair of places and that is the trouble" (OP, 158).

29. Stevens writes that poets and painters achieve their results "not by inspiration, but by imagination or by the miraculous kind of reason that the imagination sometimes promotes" (NA, 165). The distinction between reason and imagination seems as uncertain for Stevens as it was for Wordsworth.

30. Because Stevens uses blue as a part of the imagination (north-cold-moon) complex, the adjective blue "aflame" is an inconsistency which the poet recognized on reconsidering the poem. The poem, he wrote, "deals with the intensity of the imagination unmodified

by contacts with reality, if such a thing is possible. Intensity becomes something incandescent." Because "flame" is a part of the reality complex (south, sun, red, green) Stevens realized that "the metamorphosis into reality, while a good illustration, was misleading. The poem has to do with pure imagination" (*Mattino Domenicale,* p. 178).

31. "Wallace Stevens and Mallarmé," *Modern Philology,* XLIII (May, 1946), 242.

32. I believe that Hi Simons is incorrect in saying that blue "signifies much the same thing when Stevens uses it symbolically as *azure* does in its principal symbolic function for Mallarmé" ("Wallace Stevens and Mallarmé," p. 243). Far from representing the sought-for ideal, Stevens' blue is frequently rejected because it denies the ultimate value of reality.

33. Badt, *Cézanne,* p. 72.

34. *Heraclitus,* p. 103.

35. *The Principles of Art,* p. 215.

36. For example, "The gold tree is blue" (CP, 57); "The sun rises green and blue" (CP, 161); "if all the green of spring was blue, and it is" (CP, 215).

37. "Probings," p. 189.

38. Pink, red weakened by white, is employed for the most part negatively, to suggest femininity or delicacy. The "man of bitter appetite despises . . . The weather pink" (CP, 322), probably because it lacks the force of "red weather." Likewise, "The Hero in a Time of War" says, "Force is my lot and not pink-clustered/ Roma ni Avignon ni Leyden,/ And cold, my element" (CP, 273).

39. The absence of color (which for Stevens is the absence of the world) is a kind of death-in-life:

> Close the cantina. Hood the chandelier.
> The moonlight is not yellow but a white
> That silences the ever-faithful town.
> How pale and how possessed a night it is . . .
>   (CP, 144)

Yellow, however, is "first color" (CP, 431), and although it can sometimes suggest decay and dissolution ("the grass is yellow and thin" [CP, 157]), it is more often used affirmatively, linked with the sun ("The sun, in clownish yellow" [CP, 318]).

40. Michel Benamou writes: "The difference between Stevens and the French tradition hinges on the metaphysical meaning of the word *pure.* It is a contrast between feeling purity in the world, and reaching purity out of this world by an angel's flight" (Wallace Stevens and "the Symbolist Imagination," p. 107).

41. *Art and Visual Perception* (Berkeley: University of California Press, 1964), p. 297.

42. Again Stevens is distinguished from idealists like Mallarmé: "whereas Stevens enjoys the sense of the coexistence of opposites, Mallarmé expressly preferred the absent 'Otherness' to the living present" (Simons, "Wallace Stevens and Mallarmé," p. 250).

43. This interpretation runs counter to Richard Ellmann's. See "Wallace Stevens' Ice-Cream," *Kenyon Review*, XIX (Winter, 1957), 89–105.

44. Stevens' number of ways of looking is not significant. As Hillis Miller says of "Sea Surface Full of Clouds": "That there are five versions is just an accident. There might have been fifteen or twenty-five or five hundred and five" (*Poets of Reality*, p. 240).

45. Orange is used rarely by Stevens, only eleven times. For the most part it seems a positive color; "The termagant fans/ Of his orange days/ Fell, famous and flat . . ." (OP, 29).

AFTERWORD

1. Stevens concludes that his "Supreme Fiction" is "The fiction that results from feeling" (CP, 406).

2. *The Life of Forms in Art*, p. 5.

3. *The Archetypes and the Collective Unconscious*, p. 31.

4. *Language as Gesture* (London: George Allen & Unwin, Ltd., 1954), p. 226.

INDEX

252 *Index*

animals, 75–78, 140, 207–209, 222, 239n31. *See also* birds; *and see specific animals*
"Another Weeping Woman" (Stevens), 218
Apollo, 11, 23, 58; Christ and, 237n8; Heraclitus on, 169
"Apostrophe to Vincentine, The" (Stevens), 186–87, 210
Archetypal Patterns in Poetry (Bodkin), 3
"Architecture" (Stevens), 204–205
Aristotle, 51, 229
Arnheim, Rudolf, quoted, 211
"Arrival at the Waldorf" (Stevens), 24–25, 27, 106
art, *see* aesthetics; artifice; creation; *and see specific arts*
artifice, 25, 26, 29–32, 41–42, 163, 182, 235n27; allegory and, 176; art distinguished from, 146, 179, 246n14; candle image of, 80–81, 82–83, 85; church image of, 224–26; dump image and, 228–29; embroidery image of, 217; moonlight image of, 68, 97; parasol image of, 65–66; statue image of, 125–26, 129, 131, 132, 133, 136, 140–42, 143, 146, 148, 151, 154–55, 156, 168; tragedy and, 51, 52
"art symbols," defined, 7–8, 238n13, 245n1
asceticism, 6–7, 23–24, 34–35, 199, 222; Bergson on, 32; Christian, 52, 178–79, 200; Jung on, 52
"Attempt to Discover Life" (Stevens), 181–82
Auden, Wystan Hugh, quoted, 75, 102
Augustan poetry, 144

Auroras of Autumn, The (Stevens), 13–14, 23, 159, 191
autumn, 69–70, 71, 146, 150, 223, 236n5; color and, 195, 219; Keats on, 72, 128–29, 243n2
"Autumn Refrain" (Stevens), 64

"Banal Sojourn" (Stevens), 27
banjo image, 91
Bateau Ivre, Le (Rimbaud), 247n17
Battle of the Books, The (Swift), 184
Baudelaire, Charles, 99, 180, 228; quoted, 16, 183–84
Bay of Biscay, 16
Beerbohm, Max, 32
Benamou, Michel, quoted, 15–16, 69, 249n40
Bergson, Henri, quoted, 32, 36
Bible, The, 71. *See also specific Biblical figures*
"Bird with the Coppery, Keen Claws, The" (Stevens), 161
birds, 18, 20, 27, 59, 104, 129, 161, 244n15; buzzard, 26, 216; cock, 193; cockatoo, 187; colors of, 206, 210, 215; crow, 38–39; eagle, 151; jay, 164; nightingale, 64–65, 70; owl, 201–202; parakeet, 161, 166; peacock, 136, 219–20; rock image and, 170–71; turkey, 56–57, 140; Wordsworth use of, 102
Birth of Tragedy, The (Nietzsche), 11
black, 60, 143, 174, 214–20; Baudelaire use of, 184; Ellis on, 185; Eliot use of, 175; as isolation, 82, 133; roses, 181–82
Blackmur, Richard P., quoted, 39, 124, 227

256

Index

Faerie Queene, The (Spenser), 176
Fall, The, 28, 52, 93–94, 102, 188, 192, 248n27
"Farewell to Florida" (Stevens), 12, 13–15, 239n29
Faulkner, William, quoted, 168
"Figure of the Youth as Virile Poet, The" (Stevens), 244n19
"Final Soliloquy of the Interior Paramour" (Stevens), 85–86
fire imagery, 22, 60, 141–42, 159, 163, 206, 214, 244n22; blue and, 197, 248n30; green and, 23; Yeats use of, 79–80. *See also* sun imagery
"Floral Decorations for Bananas" (Stevens), 29
Florida, 12, 21, 26, 27, 125, 233n3
flowers, 14, 17, 21, 22, 29–30, 40, 143, 197, 201–202, 228; carnation, 213; garden imagery, 178, 179, 188; hyacinth, 119; mallow, 117; stone bouquet, 165, 180–81; white, 23, 70
fluctuation, 66–67, 238n16. *See also* choice; transcience
Focillon, Henri, quoted, 6, 92, 129, 131, 145–46, 226
"Forms of the Rock in a Night-Hymn" (Stevens), 171
Four Quartets (Eliot), 4, 109, 152–53, 163, 175, 223
France, 3–4, 6, 15–16, 84, 99, 249n40; Matisse chapel in, 225–26
Fraser, G. S., quoted, 5
Freud, Sigmund, 237n10
"From the Misery of Don Joost" (Stevens), 236n3
"From the Packet of Anacharsis" (Stevens), 211–12

Frost, Robert, 248n28; quoted, 45
fruit imagery, 21, 22, 29–31, 143, 192, 202, 222
Frye, Northrop, quoted, 234n4, 246n10
Fuchs, Daniel, 76; quoted, 29

Ghil, René, 241n1
"Gift, The" (Camus), 245n26
gold, 61, 66, 159, 211, 221, 223; as Christian emblem, 70, 194, 200, 239n23; Ursula and, 178, 246n12; Yeats use of, 79, 146, 206, 215
good, 38–39, 203–204
gray, 175, 178
green, 25, 28, 102, 117, 136, 144, 146, 177, 182, 183, 215, 223, 225; connotations of, 16, 20, 23–24, 126, 173–74, 185–96, 197, 198, 202, 203, 204, 207, 210, 221, 247nn21–22; Eliot use of, 176; Lear use of, 247n-16; music and, 208; rock image and, 162, 166, 167; roses, 181–82; Tindall on, 245n4; Ursula and, 178
"Greenest Continent, The" (Stevens), 142–43
Green Helmet, The (Yeats), 4
"Green Plant, The" (Stevens), 194–95
Guatemala, 24, 25
guitar motif, 47, 73; as poetry, 44, 59, 63, 88, 94–98, 105, 153, 159, 192, 197, 206, 227, 241n12, 242n13

Hamlet (Shakespeare), 51, 53, 218
Harmonium (Stevens), 5, 7, 12, 14, 47, 88, 204; earth mother in, 17, 27; moon imagery in,

Errors

p. 21
26
27
35 (debatable comma)
60
76 (debatable possessive form)
89
90
94
98
102
128 (2: misprinted <u>borne</u> + lack of stanzaic indentation)
149
187
200 (2: pantomi<u>ne</u> twice for pantomi<u>me</u>
228
251 (2: 1 debatable)
253
257
261
263
265 (2)
266 (4)

ABOUT THE AUTHOR

Edward Kessler is a graduate of the University of Virginia; he received the M.A. and Ph.D. degrees from Rutgers University and has studied at the University of Paris. His poems have appeared in the *American Scholar,* the *Saturday Review, Paris Review,* the *New Yorker, Poetry,* and other magazines.

Mr. Kessler has taught at the College of William and Mary and the University of Virginia, and he is presently on the faculty of The American University, where he teaches courses in American poetry and the Romantic Period.

The text of this book was set in Caledonia Linofilm and printed by offset on P & S Special Book LL manufactured by P. H. Glatfelter Co., Spring Grove, Pa. Composed, printed and bound by Quinn & Boden Company, Inc., Rahway, N.J. Indexed by Roberta Blaché